EXTREME FAITH

NEIL T. ANDERSON
DAVE PARK

HARVEST HOUSE PUBLISHERS
Eugene, Oregon 97402

BV
1485
.A53
1996

10|30|97

Scripture quotations are taken from the Holy Bible, New International Version ®. Copyright © 1973, 1978, 1984 by the International Bible Society. Used by permission of Zondervan Publishing House. The "NIV" and "New International Version" trademarks are registered in the United States Patent and Trademark Office by International Bible Society.

Verses marked NASB are taken from the New American Standard Bible, © 1960, 1962, 1963, 1968, 1971, 1972, 1973, 1975, 1977 by The Lockman Foundation. Used by permission.

Verses marked NKJV are taken from the New King James Version, Copyright © 1979, 1980, 1982 by Thomas Nelson, Inc., Publishers. Used by permission.

Portions of this book were taken from *Victory of Darkness* and *Living Free in Christ* by Neil Anderson, published by Gospel Light Publishers, Oxnard, CA. Used by permission.

EXTREME FAITH

Copyright © 1996 Harvest House Publishers
Eugene, Oregon 97402

ISBN 1-56507-340-1

Printed in the United States of America.

96 97 98 99 00 01 02 03 — 10 9 8 7 6 5 4 3 2

#34646397

Dedicated to

David Park and Karl Anderson, our sons. As your fathers we always love you. You please us with your presence. We brag about you when you're not around, and we can't believe God has blessed us with sons like you. We hope and pray that you will walk free in Christ all the days of your lives and experience His matchless love and acceptance. We also pray that as your dads we will model that love and acceptance for you. Dave and Karl, We love you.

Acknowledgments

We want to thank all of the staff at Freedom in Christ Ministries. Special thanks to Roger McNichols, Rich Miller, Larry Beckner, Jim Wern, Dawson Grover and Dan Roelofs. And a really, really special thanks to their wives who let them travel, work extra hours, take phone calls at odd hours, and put up with all the challenges of ministry. Debby, Shirley, Joyce, Donna, Karen, and Tammy—thanks for putting up with us! Most of all, we want to thank our wives, Grace and Joanne; the joy and love you bring to our lives cannot be measured. You truly demonstrate what true freedom in Christ is.

To the whole Harvest House team: Thanks for loving youth and caring enough about them to provide valuable resources that direct them to their freedom in Christ.

Contents

How to Use This Book

from those lies. The enemy is crafty. He isn't about to simply give up his efforts to tempt, accuse, and deceive you. But in Christ we have authority to keep the enemy at bay and uncover any hidden lies we might be believing. This book will help you maintain your walk of freedom.

In order for God to use this devotional study to help you break stubborn habits and expose the enemy's lies, you need to get involved by answering the questions. The questions will get you in the Word of God, the truth. Spending time with God on a daily basis is not how Satan wants you to spend your time. He knows that if he can keep you from God's Word, he can keep you from growing in Christ. Satan can't stop us from getting to know Jesus better—unless we let him; that's a privilege everyone is entitled to. If you're experiencing unusual tiredness, a wandering mind, or the inability to concentrate, you may be under attack! You need to exercise the authority you have in Christ or get more sleep.

So, before you begin to study, verbally "submit yourselves, then, to God. Resist the devil, and he will flee from you" (James 4:7). Ask God to speak to you through His Word and help you to understand it. The Holy Spirit was given to each of us to help us understand truth; be sure to ask for His help!

Getting Started

1. Pray for God's protection against the enemy and pray for God's understanding.

2. Study the key verses used each day, then look them up in your Bible to catch the context.

3. Look up and read each of the Scripture references. How do they relate to you personally? Write out your comments and insights.

4. Answer each of the reflection questions. How do they relate to your life?

5. State out loud the *lie to reject*, the *truth to accept*, and the *prayer*. And be sure to check out the Extreme Extras. This is the place where you can explore God's Word more deeply. Use the express yourself section to answer the reflection questions, or just put down your thoughts regarding what you're learning. If you need extra room, pick up a spiral notebook.

6. In addition to reading and studying the Scripture references in the daily devotional, you need to read and study whole sections of God's Word. We strongly recommend that you read through the book of Luke in conjunction with this study! There is a 40-day reading outline for Luke on page 244, to help you set your own study pace.

Also, we strongly recommend you read *Stomping Out the Darkness* and the *Bondage Breaker (Youth Edition)* to prepare for this book. We hope you have already taken time to hear from the Lord and gone through the Steps to

Freedom. This devotional will help you renew your

a quiet place
and distractions (like the television or radio) to bug you.

Make yourself accountable to someone: a trusted friend, youth pastor, brother or sister, maybe even your mom or dad. Ask this person to monitor your progress. It would be helpful if both of you are doing this study together.

Our prayer is that this book would point you to the love, acceptance, freedom, and joy that Jesus gives to His followers. We pray God will open up many ministry opportunities for you to share the truths found in this book. May God bless your time with Him.

—Neil & Dave

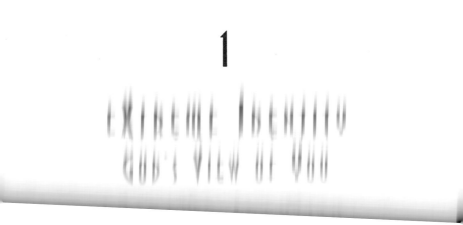

1

Do you ever feel like you're a product of your past? That because of your sins you have little or no hope of ever living the truly victorious Christian life? If so, you're not alone. Over 70 percent of the Christian teenagers we have surveyed feel as you do. They tell themselves, "I'm no good," "I can't do anything right," "Christianity may work for others, but it doesn't work for me." But according to Colossians 3:10,11, how we identified ourselves before we accepted Christ no longer applies.

When asked to describe yourself, you may mention your race, religion, cultural background, social distinction, or all the sins you committed before you accepted Christ. But Paul is saying your identity is no longer determined by your physical heritage, social standing, racial distinctions, or sins. Your identity lies in the fact that you are a child of God and are *in Christ.*

When you decided to put your trust in Christ, you gained forgiveness from every sin you would ever commit because Christ died once for *all* our sins (Romans 6:10). You received the Holy Spirit and a brand-new eternal life in Christ. Your deepest identity is that of a saint, a child of God, a divine masterpiece, a child of light, a citizen of heaven.

"You are a chosen people, a royal priesthood, a holy nation, a people belonging to God, that you may declare the praises of him who called you out of darkness into his wonderful light. Once you were not a people, but now you are the people of God; once you had not received mercy, but now you have received mercy" (1 Peter 2:9,10).

My (Dave's) brother-in-law Matt was adopted by the DuPeire family. He made a decision to trust Christ at an early age. Life in a Christian home was good and his new mom and dad truly loved him; he was their son. But something in us desires to know our roots; when Matt turned 18 he wanted to find out more about his family heritage. He researched his adoption records and what he discovered wasn't heartwarming. His mother had abandoned him and his younger brother and sister at an old hotel and put them up for adoption. Five "could be" fathers signed his adoption papers.

So, now that Matt knew the truth about his earthly family, what did it do to his heritage, his identity? Nothing. Why? Because Matt is still a child of God. The truth of 2 Corinthians 5:17 will never change: "Therefore, if anyone is in Christ, he is a new creation; the old has gone, the new has come!"

We are no longer products of our past but products of Christ's work on the cross. When we were dead in our trespasses and sins, we learned to live our lives independent of God. Our identity and perception of ourselves were formed and programmed into our minds through the natural order of this world. That's why Paul says in Romans 12:2: "Do not conform any longer to the pattern of this world, but be transformed by the renewing of your mind. Then you will be able to test and approve what God's will is—his good, pleasing and perfect will."

Renewing our minds does not come naturally; there is no automatic "delete button" that erases past programming.

We have to consciously know the Word of God so that we

of God, and what we will be has not yet been made known. But we know that when he appears, we shall be like him, for we shall see him as he is. Everyone who has this hope in him purifies himself, just as he is pure.

Each day take some time to let the Lord speak to you. Let Him reveal to your mind any lies you need to renounce and any truths you need to accept. It's our prayer that this book will strengthen your walk with Christ or be the beginning of a new habit—getting in God's Word. Be sure to meditate on the Bible passages and answer the questions.

Say the following statements out loud:

THE LIE TO REJECT:

I reject the lie that I can find lasting significance, safety, security, and a sense of belonging from anyone or anything other than Jesus Christ.

THE TRUTH TO ACCEPT:

I accept the truth that in Christ I am already significant, safe, and secure in Him: I belong to Him and am part of the family of God.

PRAYER FOR TODAY:

Dear heavenly Father, Thank You that I am not just a product of my past, but a product of Christ's good work. I know my sins have been paid for by the precious blood of Jesus Christ and that He has declared me righteous. I choose not to get my eternal significance, security, and belonging from the world; but, rather, I accept what Jesus says about me. Help me, Lord, not to conform any longer to the pattern of this world, but to be transformed by the renewing of my mind. I want to be able to do God's will, whatever is good, pleasing and perfect. In Jesus' name I pray. Amen.

DAY TWO

"Then you will know the truth, and the truth will set you free." They answered him, "We are Abraham's descendants and have never been slaves of anyone. How can you say that we shall be set free?" Jesus replied, "I tell you the truth, everyone who sins is a slave to sin. Now a slave has no permanent place in the family, but a son belongs to it forever. So if the Son sets you free, you will be free indeed (John 8:32–36).

Who are you? It's an important question; your answer will reveal what you believe about yourself, and how you feel about yourself. Take time now to answer that question: Who are you?

portant because it controls how we act. For example, if you believe you're ugly and stupid, you're less likely to take care of your body and to try as hard in your studies. You develop the kind of attitude that says, "What's the point?" If you view yourself as a sin-sick sinner, how do you think you'll live? You will probably sin more! "For as he thinks within himself, so he is" (Proverbs 23:7 NASB).

We tend to get our identity from how we look or what we do. But is who you are determined by what you do, or is what you do determined by who you are?

The second statement is true! Our identity comes from what Jesus did for us, not what we can do for Him. If you think about it, what can we really do for Jesus that doesn't come from the power of God's Holy Spirit? John 15:5 says, "I am the vine; you are the branches. If a man remains in me and I in him, he will bear much fruit; apart from me you can do nothing." Our hope for growth, meaning and fulfillment as Christians is based not on our academic abilities or athletic accomplishments but on understanding who we are as children of God. Second Corinthians 5:16,17 tells us: "From now on we recognize no man according to the flesh; even though we have known Christ according to the flesh, yet now we know Him thus no longer. Therefore if any man is in Christ, he is a new creature; the old things passed away; behold, new things have come."

Lyle Alzado was one of the toughest men who had ever played football. As a defensive end for the Raiders, he was like a heat-seeking missile; with his strength and speed, he could lock onto whoever had the ball, and he usually left the other guy drilled into the ground. Two times he was made All-Pro.

To make the Raider team, you have to play like a crazed animal and do whatever it takes to win. At first, Lyle thought he would never make the team; he only weighed 195 pounds, and while that may seem like a lot to us, at that size, he simply couldn't make it in the NFL. So Lyle decided to take steroids and work out like a man with a mission. Soon he was a monstrous 300-pound defensive machine.

No one can question Lyle's heart. His drive and desire is seldom matched even in the ranks of professionals. But Lyle made some poor choices. His decision to take steroids brought him success and fame, but only for a short time. The drugs transformed Lyle's body into a mountain of muscle, but it is also believed that those same chemicals brought on the brain cancer that ended his life. Lyle Alzado died in 1992 at only 43 years old— his life was literally cut in half. He thought playing football would make him somebody special and bring him the importance and meaning he longed for. What if Lyle had never played football? Would his wife and family still love him? Of course. His football success wasn't worth dying for.

We are complete people and our lives are extremely important because of what Christ did on the cross. If you are looking to anyone or anything other than Christ to have? Give examples, both good and bad.

Why do you think Satan would want to deceive you when it comes to your identity in Christ?

Say the following statements out loud:

THE LIE TO REJECT:

I reject the lie that my identity comes through what I do or what people say about me!

THE TRUTH TO ACCEPT:

I accept the truth that my identity comes through what Christ did for me on the cross and what He says about me!

PRAYER FOR TODAY:

Dear heavenly Father, How awesome it is that I can call You Father. Thank You for the truth that I'm not identified by the things I do, but rather by what Christ did for me. Thank You for placing me in Christ, and that I am a new creature—that the old things in my life have passed away, and the new things have come. Lord, help me have the right identity equations in my life. Reveal any lies I might be believing about who I am, and remind me daily to affirm the truth about my identity in You. In Jesus' name I pray. Amen.

——————— DAY THREE ———————

For you were once darkness, but now you are light in the Lord. Live as children of light (for the fruit of the light consists in all goodness, righteousness and truth) and find out what pleases the Lord (Ephesians 5:8-10).

In order to understand who you are, you need to understand what you inherited—good and bad—from Adam at the time of creation. Just as you inherited physical traits from your parents, you also inherited certain traits from your first father, Adam.

Genesis 2:7 says: "The Lord God formed man from the dust of the ground and breathed into his nostrils the breath of life, and man became a living being." God created Adam. Like Adam, you have a physical body and an inner self. Your physical body relates to the world around you through your five senses, while your inner self, sometimes called your soul, is that part of you created in the image of God. Your mind, emotions, and will are all part of your inner self and out of them you think, feel, and make choices. These parts of you are meant to be spiritually connected to God.

At creation, Adam was both physically and spiritually alive: physically alive because his body was in union with his soul, and spiritually alive because his soul was in union with God. Your physical body is important, but your greatest focus should be your spiritual life because sins. However, when you accepted Christ as a sacrifice for your sins, your soul was brought back into union with God, and your spiritual life was restored. Spiritual union with God meets four important needs: Acceptance—knowing that God loves you unconditionally; significance—knowing your real purpose in life; safety and security—knowing God will take care of you forever; and belonging—knowing you are part of God's eternal family.

Acceptance, significance, safety and security, and belonging are important needs. Which of these is the greatest need in your life today?

How did God provide acceptance, significance, safety and security, and belonging for Adam and Eve? Check out Genesis 1:26,27 to see how He provided them with acceptance and a sense of significance; Genesis 1:29,30 to see how He provided safety and security; and Genesis 2:18 to see how He provided them with a sense of belonging.

Romans 5:12 says, "Therefore, just as sin entered the world through one man, and death through sin, and in this way death came to all men, because all sinned—"

The effect of man's fall was devastating. When sin entered the human race and was passed on to you, it brought about four spiritual flaws. First, Adam and Eve lost their *knowledge of God*; they tried to hide from an all-knowing

God who is everywhere (Genesis 3:7-9). They were experiencing some serious brain cramps!

When my (Dave's) little girl Dani was three years old, she liked to play hide and seek. The problem was that after she would hide she would yell out, "I'm ready!" As you might guess, it wasn't hard to find her. She had no knowledge of how sound waves could pinpoint her hiding place. Adam's and Eve's effort to hide from God demonstrated just how much knowledge they had lost. Sadly, what Adam and Eve lost, you and I never had until we found Christ.

Not only did the fall affect our thinking, it affected our emotions as well. Our second flaw is *dominant negative emotions*. When Adam and Eve sinned, the first emotions they expressed were guilt and shame (see Genesis 3:7), then fear (see Genesis 3:8).

The third flaw relates to your choices. Because of the fall you now have *too many choices*. Sin affected Adam's and Eve's will. In the Garden of Eden they could only make one wrong choice. Everything they wanted to do was okay, except eating from the tree of the knowledge of good and evil (see Genesis 2:16,17). As a result of their sin, you are bombarded with a ton of good and bad choices every day.

The final flaw was *spiritual death*. Adam and Eve lost their relationship with God; they were cut off from Him. Now every human being who comes into the world is born physically alive but spiritually dead (see Ephesians 2:1).

Because of the fall you'll experience rejection, guilt, shame, and feel weak and helpless at times. There is a way out of our problems, however. Adam was followed by the last "Adam," Jesus Christ. He won back we all lost in the Garden of Eden?

Say the following statements out loud:

The Lie to Reject:

I reject the lie that my identity comes from the first Adam and his sin. I am not identified as a sinner, but as a saint.

The Truth to Accept:

I accept the truth that my identity only comes from the second Adam, Jesus Christ, who never sinned, and that I am spiritually alive in Christ and seated in heavenly places with Him forever.

Prayer for Today:

Dear heavenly Father, I have experienced rejection, guilt, and shame, and at times I've felt weak and helpless. I know this is because of the fall of mankind and sin in my life. Thank You for providing a way out of my problems. I realize that I could not have any relationship with You on the basis of my own works. But I thank You that in Christ I am forgiven and have eternal life. I no longer want to identify myself with the first Adam, but rather with the last Adam, Jesus Christ. I accept the love and acceptance I have in Him. In Jesus' name I pray. Amen.

——————DAY FOUR——————

To the Church of God which is at Corinth, to those who have been sanctified in Christ Jesus, saints by calling, with all who in every place call upon the name of our Lord Jesus Christ, their Lord and ours (1 Corinthians 1:2).

Take note, sometime, of how often the Bible identifies Christians as "saints." The word "saint" literally means "holy person." The writers of the New Testament used the word "saint" to describe common, everyday believers like us. Like you!

Some people have bought into the idea that we can earn the lofty title of saint by living a good life or reaching a certain level of maturity. But Paul didn't say we were saints because of hard work. He clearly states that we are "saints by calling." We are saints because God calls us saints, and because we are alive in Christ.

Many Christians claim, "I'm just a sinner saved by grace." But are we really sinners? No, that's what we were before we accepted Christ. God doesn't call us sinners; He calls us saints—holy ones, children of God who are spiritually alive. If you think you're a sinner, guess what you'll do—you will probably live like a sinner; you will sin. You may say, "But I still sin once in awhile, doesn't that make fell to his death. As the sad story unfolded, people began to report that he had predicted his fall. He had the feeling he was going to fall. Remember, how we think determines how we behave (see Proverbs 23:7). Wallenda believed he was going to fall and what happened? He fell. What we believe affects how we live. Satan can't do anything to damage our position and identity in Christ. But if he can deceive us into believing his lie—that we're no-good sinners and that God doesn't accept us—then we will live as if we have no position or identity in Christ. Don't believe what the world or the devil says about you. Believe what Jesus says about you; He's the one who is telling the truth. He knows the true you!

We are all saints by the grace of God, sanctified because we are in Christ Jesus. Every child of God is a saint because he is *in* Christ Jesus. We have a tremendous inheritance in Christ. "Praise be to the God and Father of our Lord Jesus Christ, who has blessed us in the heavenly realms with every spiritual blessing *in Christ*. For he chose us *in him* before the creation of the world" (Ephesians 1:3,4, emphasis added).

In the book of Ephesians, 40 references are made to you being in Christ or Christ dwelling in you. And for every verse in the Bible that talks about Christ being in you, you can find 10 verses that talk about you being in Him. Go through the rest of Ephesians 1 and see how many times you find this truth. In verse 7, you find, "*In him* we have redemption." In verse 11, it says, "*In him* we were also chosen." Verse 12 tells you that your hope lies *in Christ*. Verse 13 says you were included *in Christ* when you heard the word of truth.

The incredible work of Christ's redemption is what makes you a saint. Our old self is replaced by something that did not exist in us before. We are declared a new creation (see 2 Corinthians 5:17; Galatians 6:15). This newness of life is the life of Jesus Christ within the believer (see Galatians 2:20; Colossians 3:3). You become one spirit with the Lord (see 1 Corinthians 6:17). In the practice of daily living, the Christian is told to "put on the new self" (Ephesians 4:24). By faith, we are to function in the light of our true identity—who we really are in Christ Jesus.

Paul identifies the believer with Christ:

In His death	Romans 6:3,6; Galatians 2:20; Colossians 3:1-3
In His burial	Romans 6:4
In His resurrection	Romans 6:5,8,11
In His life	Romans 5:10,11
In His power	Ephesians 1:19,20
In His inheritance	Romans 8:16,17; Ephesians 1:11,12

God calls you a saint. That awesome truth should overpower the lies that the world and Satan want you to believe. Can you identify any lies or deceptions about yourself that may have been thrown at you by the enemy?

Renounce the lies out loud. Don't let the enemy blind you to the truth of your awesome identity!

Spirit who calls out, 'Abba, Father.' So you are no longer a slave, but a son; and since you are a son, God has made you also an heir." In other words, you have a bonding relationship with your heavenly Father. This may be the primary role of the Holy Spirit. "The Spirit himself testifies with our spirit that we are God's children" (Romans 8:16).

What truths about your identity can you throw back at Satan when he accuses you and tempts you to believe his deceptions about who you are?

On one side of a 3x5-inch card, write out a lie that Satan wants you to believe. Now, on the other side, write out one of the truths from the "Who Am I" list (page 205), that best destroys Satan's lie. Take more cards and write out at least five more lies and the answering truth.

The Lie to Reject:

I reject the lie that I am just a sinner, and that I have to sin or go back to the way things were before I accepted Christ.

The Truth to Accept:

I accept the truth that I am a saint, a holy one in Christ Jesus and free to obey Him.

PRAYER FOR TODAY:

Dear heavenly Father, I have renounced the lie that I am a sinner. I acknowledge that I truly am a saint, a holy one—not because of anything that I have done, but because of what Jesus did for me when He redeemed me from my sins. I choose by faith to receive my true identity as a saint. I ask You to fill me with Your Holy Spirit and enable me to live out my true identity as a child of Yours so I may not sin. I want to walk in the truth and not follow or believe any deceptions from the enemy so that I may glorify You. I pray this in Jesus' name. Amen.

DAY FIVE

But because of his great love for us, God, who is rich in mercy, made us alive with Christ even when we were dead in transgressions—it is by grace you have been saved. And God raised us up with Christ and seated us with him in the heavenly realms in Christ Jesus (Ephesians 2:4-6).

A few years ago, I (Neil) was invited to speak at a bookseller's convention. There was a dinner preceding my talk, and those of us seated at the head table were asked to show up early so we could be instructed in how we were to enter. We marched into the room to the tune of "When the Saints Go Marching In." We then stood side-by-side behind the table until the master of ceremonies stated, "Ladies and gentlemen, this is your head

Christ in the heavenly realm? The riches of His grace are incomparable. That He would give us such a privilege is beyond comprehension! Do you see the incredible kindness of our Lord in saying to a beggar who has known only rejection, "Come, sit with me at my right hand"?

The right hand position by God's throne is the center of authority and power for the whole universe. That power was given our ascended Lord. The elevation of His people with Him to the heavenlies means that we share His authority. We are made to sit with Him as heirs. "The Spirit himself testifies with our spirit that we are God's children. Now if we are children, then we are heirs—heirs of God and co-heirs with Christ, if indeed we share in his sufferings in order that we may also share in his glory" (Romans 8:16,17).

The significance of this can't be overstated. You may feel as though you are caught between two equal and opposite forces—Satan on one side and God on the other. If you believe this is a true picture, you are misled. The truth is that God is all knowing, all powerful, and kind and loving in all His ways. Satan is a defeated foe, and we are in Christ, seated with Him in the heavenlies. Notice the parallel account in Colossians 2:9-11,13-15:

> For in Christ all the fullness of the Deity
> lives in bodily form, and you have been given

fullness *in Christ*, who is the head over every power and authority. *In him* you were also circumcised, in the putting off of the sinful nature. . . . When you were dead in your sins and in the uncircumcision of your sinful nature, God made you alive with Christ. He forgave us all our sins, having canceled the written code, with its regulations, that was against us and that stood opposed to us; he took it away, nailing it to the cross. And having disarmed the powers and authorities, he made a public spectacle of them, triumphing over them by the cross (emphasis added).

We can only delegate responsibility when we have authority to carry it out. Because we are seated with Christ, we have authority over the kingdom of darkness. But our authority is not independent. We don't have the authority to do whatever we want. This is not an authority over each other either, because we are to "submit to one another out of reverence for Christ" (Ephesians 5:21). What we do have is the authority to do God's will.

In 1969, a certain doctor was researching a terrible catatonic disease sometimes referred to as the sleeping disease. This disease caused its victims to shake uncontrollably until finally it left them in a frozen state. Like statues, they would sit immovable. What was worse, their minds shut down as well; they couldn't remember the simplest detail of their lives. They were unable to speak or feed themselves. But one day this doctor experimented with a synthetic drug called El-Dopa. What happened next was incredible. The patients who were given the drug experienced what the doctor called an awakening. They could speak, move freely, and remember everything. Sadly, are moved. They're on fire for the Lord, but only for a short time. Soon they go back to old ways of thinking and believing. Why? Too many young Christians identify with the first Adam—with the Adam who sinned. But those who have trusted Christ are no longer identified with Adam and his sin—but with Jesus and His righteousness. We are not locked outside God's presence as Adam was. We are seated with Christ in the heavenly places. The difference between Adam and Christ is eternally profound. Who are you identifying with?

Our spiritual relationship with God is complete and eternal because it is provided by Christ. The Christian life is not a series of brief awakenings. When you were born spiritually, God wrote your name in Jesus' book of life and you became a citizen of heaven (see Revelation 21:27). As long as Christ remains alive spiritually, we will remain alive spiritually—and that's forever.

What does the phrase "in Christ" mean to you? How does it affect the way you live your life day to day?

What does it mean to be spiritually alive in Christ?

How does seeing yourself as a child of God seated in the heavenlies with Christ enable you to better live the Christian life?

The Lie to Reject:

I reject the lie that I have no power or authority over Satan and his cohorts.

The Truth to Accept:

I accept the truth that in Christ I have power and authority over sin and Satan.

Prayer for Today:

Dear Heavenly Father, I can hardly believe that You would allow me the honor of sitting at Your right hand. But I know Your Word is true so how can I doubt? There is no greater position of honor than this, yet You have given it to me. Lord, I thank You for Your kindness. Thank You for the power and authority You have given me in Christ. I renounce the lie of Satan that I have no authority over him. I know, Lord, that I have no authority apart from You, but I acknowledge that I have authority in Christ because I am seated with Him in the heavenly realms.

Write out what these verses say about you.

(Matthew 5:13,14): _____

(John 1:12): _____

(John 15:1,5,15,16): _____

(Acts 1:8): _____

(Romans 6:18,22): _____

(Romans 8:14,15): _____

(Galatians 3:26; 4:6): _____

(Ephesians 6:10): _____

EXPAND YOUR MIND

Memorize John 1:12:

> Yet to all who received Him, to those who
> believed in His name, He gave the right to be-
> come children of God.

Express Yourself

2

BEYOND GENERATION X
HOW YOU VIEW YOURSELF

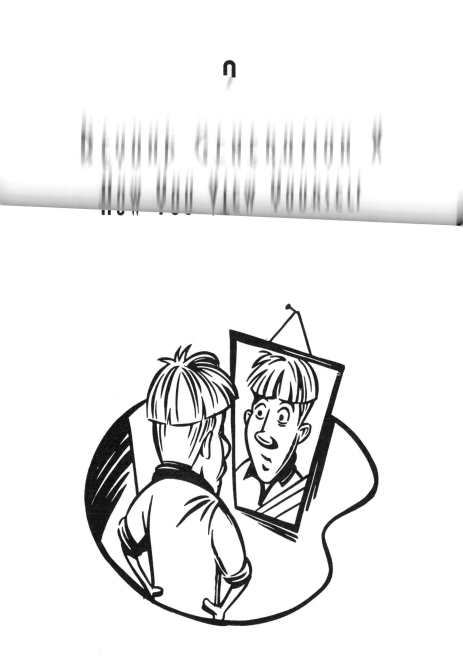

fill the great commission. Your generation is the most likely to see Christ return. God is calling your generation to bring about real and lasting revival to His body, the church. That doesn't sound like Generation X to us.

The world would like to reject this generation. Rejection is one of the most painful experiences known to humanity. Years ago, I (Neil) was having a devotional time with my children and raised the question, "What is rejection?" My daughter, Heidi, gave a nice answer, but my son, Karl, followed by nailing the issue right on the heart. He said, "I know. Rejection is when Johnny won't play with me anymore and I have to play with Heidi." Unconditional love and acceptance is one of the most basic needs of humanity. Yet, often, the world tells the Christian in no uncertain terms, "You're not welcome here. You're not wanted or needed."

Have you ever noticed how little kids strive to get your acceptance and approval? "Do you like my picture?" they ask a hundred times. "See what I can do!" The social system in which most of us were raised programmed us to believe that if we appeared good, performed well, or possessed a certain amount of social status, we would be somebody. But try as we might to gain approval, we always come up short. Whatever pinnacle of self-identity we are able to achieve eventually crumbles under the pressure of rejection or the criticism of self-condemnation. We cannot do anything to qualify for unconditional and voluntary love. We labor under the false assumption that if we live perfectly everybody will accept us, while there was one who lived perfectly, and many people rejected Him.

Understanding and receiving God's unconditional love is basic for all future growth. We don't have to do anything to gain God's acceptance; we are completely accepted by God as we are. Our actions and works should be in response to God's love, not an attempt to earn His favor.

Finding our acceptance in Christ serves as a foundation for our relationship with other people as well. Paul writes in Romans 15:7, "Accept one another, then, just as Christ accepted you, in order to bring praise to God."

Our need for acceptance and belonging are legitimate needs; they are God-given. But if we attempt to get them met independently of God, we are doomed to reap the dissatisfaction the self-life brings. Peter admonishes us to lay aside the relentless pursuit of the approval of man:

> Therefore, rid yourselves of all malice and all deceit, hypocrisy, envy, and slander of every kind. Like newborn babies, crave pure spiritual milk, so that by it you may grow up in your salvation, now that you have tasted that the Lord is good. As you come to him, the living Stone—rejected by men but chosen by God and precious to him—you also, like living stones, are being built into a spiritual house to be a holy priesthood (1 Peter 2:1-5).

Malice is wicked behavior that seeks to put others down in order to get our own way! It is often born out of to gain approval. When this fails, their envy of those who seem to have what they don't have causes them to slander and hurt the person they envy. So strong and devious is man's inner craving for significance apart from Christ!

But when you know who you are in Christ, you no longer need to be threatened by people or compete with them, because you are already loved and accepted.

The newborn baby knows nothing about guile, hypocrisy, and envy. In reality, Christians are like babies; newborn in Christ, we long for the pure milk of the Word because it is there we discover our true identity. Sure, we will sometimes experience the rejection of people, but our heavenly Father will never cast us away. He has promised to never leave us nor forsake us.

THE LIE TO REJECT:

I reject the lie that I am unaccepted or that I must earn God's love and approval.

THE TRUTH TO ACCEPT:

I accept the truth that God loves and accepts me unconditionally.

PRAYER FOR TODAY:

Dear heavenly Father, I pray that You would open my eyes so I may know and personally receive Your unconditional love and acceptance. I renounce the lies of Satan that question Your love and insist I must earn Your love and approval. I choose to believe that I am accepted in Christ. I ask for Your grace to sustain me as I face the rejection of people. Please enable me to stand against the peer pressure that tempts me to compromise. In Jesus' precious name I pray. Amen.

—————— DAY SEVEN ——————

Yet to all who received him, to those who believed in his name, he gave the right to become children of God—children born not of natural descent, nor of human decision or a husband's will, but born of God (John 1:12,13).

You are a child of God; this is a right given to you by God.

When I (Dave) watched my first child come into the world, I decided to give him my name, first and last. Not only does little Dave have my name, but he has my blood flowing through his veins. Is there anything little Dave could possibly do to change his blood relationship with me, his father? What if he ran away from home and changed his name? What if he disowned me? Would he with God. You're related to Him through the blood of Christ: "You know that it was not with perishable things such as silver or gold that you were redeemed from the empty way of life handed down to you from your forefathers, but with the precious blood of Christ, a lamb without blemish or defect" (1 Peter 1:18,19). Your fellowship will suffer when you disobey His will, but you have been born again into the family of God. You are forever God's child. He will always love and accept you. When you sin you don't need to reaccept Christ, you simply need to get your fellowship back in order by confessing your sin and renouncing the way you behaved (see 1 John 1:9).

So where should you place your effort in the process of spiritual growth and maturity? Not on your relationship to God, because you can do nothing to improve upon it; you can only continue to believe that it is true. You are a child of God if you have received Him into your life by faith—period. Rather, work on your fellowship with God; determine in your heart to believe what He says is true and obey Him. The result will be true spiritual growth and peace with God as you grow and fellowship with Him.

I could choose to disobey and no longer live in harmony with my heavenly Father, but that would not affect our blood relationship. And as long as you choose to believe the truth and respond by faith in obedience to God you will live in harmony with Him. Making these distinctions is critical. If I thought it was my obedience that determined whether or not I would stay related to God, I would be subjecting myself again to legalism. I would logically conclude that if I disobeyed God I would lose my relationship with Him. But that's not true; we are saved by grace, through faith, not by works. On the other hand, there are those who glibly say, "I know God will never leave me," but they fail to live a victorious life because they don't obey Him. But Jesus says, "'If anyone loves me, he will obey my teaching'" (John 14:23).

We are not saved by how we *behave*. We are saved by how we *believe*. When we enter into a relationship with God by faith, we can exclaim with John, "How great is the love the Father has lavished on us, that we should be called children of God! And that is what we are! . . . Dear friends, now we are children of God, and what we will be has not yet been made known. But we know that when he appears, we shall be like him, for we shall see him as he is. Everyone who has this hope in him purifies himself, just as he is pure" (1 John 3:1-3).

This important passage drives home once again how critical it is to know who we are as children of God, because it serves as the basis for how we live our lives. How we perceive ourselves will have a powerful effect on how we live our lives.

When Jesus instructed the disciples to pray, how did He start? He started with "Our Father." This is the most important inward, personal thing we can say as we address God. And if He is our Father, then we must be His children. Do you have this assurance? If not, settle it now, once and for all.

If you aren't

into my heart. I receive You into my life. I believe that Jesus died for my sin, was raised on the third day, and I confess with my mouth that Jesus is Lord.

After accepting Christ, why does our personal sin affect our fellowship with God and not our relationship with Him?

How can you enrich your fellowship with your heavenly Father?

The Lie to Reject:

I reject the lie that I can lose my salvation when I fail to live in perfect faith and obedience, or that my relationship with God will be severed because of my sin.

The Truth to Accept:

I accept the truth that nothing can separate me from the love of God, and that I am forever His child through the blood of Christ.

Prayer for Today:

I come to You as Your child. I thank You for giving me eternal life. I renounce any lie of

Satan that says I have no right to be called Your child, and I thank You that You give me that right. I no longer put any confidence in myself; my confidence is in You and in the fact that I am saved, not by what I have done, but by what You have done through Christ on the cross. I accept myself as a child of God because of the free gift You have given me. I gladly receive it and accept it for all eternity. In Jesus' name I pray. Amen.

Day Eight

. . . giving thanks to the Father, who has qualified you to share in the inheritance of the saints in the kingdom of light. For he has rescued us from the dominion of darkness and brought us into the kingdom of the Son he loves, in whom we have redemption, the forgiveness of sins (Colossians 1:12-14).

In Christ you are declared righteous and are completely accepted by God. But if that's true, why is our behavior less than perfect? Why do we sometimes sin? Paul wrote in Romans 7:19, "For what I do is not the good I want to do; no, the evil I do not want to do—this I keep on doing." It's clear we sin, so are we saints or not? What is our true nature?

God declares that you "are not in the flesh but in the Spirit" (Romans 8:9 NASB). You are one or the other, not half and half. Ephesians 5:8 states, "You were once darkness, but now you are light in the Lord. Live as children of light." Darkness and light are not fighting for control within you. When ~~...~~

~~...~~ part darkness,
part saint and part sinner, you'll live an unfruitful life with
little to distinguish you from the non-Christian. You may
confess your tendency to sin and strive to do better, but
you will live out a continually defeated life because you'll
think of yourself as a sinner who is just hanging on until
Jesus comes.

Satan knows he can do nothing about who you really
are in Christ. But if he can get you to believe you are no
different than the non-Christian, you will behave no
differently.

God's work in changing sinners to saints is one of His
greatest accomplishments on earth. Your inner change
(justification), when God took away your sin and gave
you His righteousness, happened the moment you
trusted Christ. The outer change (sanctification), learning
to think and act like Christ, continues throughout life.
You must accept the truth that you are a new creation in
order to live out the truly Spirit-filled life.

When you came into a spiritual relationship or union
with God through your new birth, you didn't add a new,
divine nature to your old, sinful nature. You *exchanged*
natures. You were, by nature, children of wrath (Ephesians 2:1-3); now you are a partaker of the divine nature
(2 Peter 1:4). Salvation is more than forgiveness of sins
and a free ticket to heaven when you die. *Salvation is not*

addition, it is complete transformation. God changed you from darkness to light, from sinner to saint. There is a newness about you that wasn't there before. If God hadn't changed who you were at salvation, you would be nothing but a product of your past. Receiving God's nature is basic to your identity and maturity in Christ.

As a new Christian, you were like a lump of coal: unattractive, messy to work with, and somewhat fragile. With time and pressure, however, coal becomes hardened and beautiful. Even though the original lump of coal is not a diamond, it consists of the necessary substance to become a diamond. You're not a mixture of natures or a partaker of two natures, but rather a partaker of one divine nature. You are not fully sanctified yet—that is, you don't fully resemble Christ in every area of your life right now. But the process of becoming more like Christ has begun because the right substance (the new nature) is present in you.

The issue is not to improve your old nature—that is already settled. The issue is to learn how to walk in harmony with your new nature. "Those who belong to Christ Jesus have crucified the sinful nature with its passions and desires" (Galatians 5:24). The presence of your new nature allows you to not only act like Christ, but to *be* like Christ.

So, we don't become Christians by acting like Christians. We are not on a performance basis with God. He knows we can't solve the problem of our old sinful self by simply improving our behavior. He knew He had to change our very nature—who we are—and give us an entirely new self, the life of Christ in us.

THE LIE TO REJECT

... the truth that I have been rescued from the domain of darkness and placed into the kingdom of Jesus, that I am a saint because of Jesus' work on the cross. I accept the truth that my old self was crucified with Christ and that I no longer have to be subject to sin's power over me.

PRAYER FOR TODAY:

Dear heavenly Father, I believe what Your Word says about me even though it seems too good to be true. I choose not to let Satan trick me into believing that I am still in darkness and that I have to sin. I choose to say no to sin and yes to You and walk in Your light. I want to believe You, Lord, and Your Word. Lord, thank You for Your grace and the gift of an entirely new life. I know that, apart from the spirit-controlled life and nature, I would be powerless to become the child You want me to be. Teach me how to walk in the Spirit by faith. I choose not to violate my new nature and my new identity by serving self. Help me, Lord, not to act independent of You, but to follow Your ways. In Jesus, name I pray. Amen.

Day Nine

Since, then, you have been raised with Christ, set your hearts on things above, where Christ is seated at the right hand of God. Set your minds on things above, not on earthly things. For you died, and your life is now hidden with Christ in God (Colossians 3:1-3).

Do you ever feel like you're the only Christian on the whole planet who is struggling? And everybody else seems to have their spiritual act together? Well, Satan likes it when we think that way, because it isolates us and makes us afraid to ask others for help. Satan loves to trick us into thinking only weak people need help. He says things like, "True Christians never struggle" or "If you're struggling, you're not a Christian." But we all need God and we desperately need each other.

A pastor visited me (Neil) a few years ago, and confessed, "I've struggled to live a victorious Christian life for 20 years. I know what my problem is—Colossians 3:3 says: `For you died, and your life is now hidden with Christ in God.' I've struggled all these years because I haven't died like this verse says. How do I do that, Neil?"

"Dying is not your problem," I said. "Read the verse again, a little slower."

"'For you died, and your life is now hidden with Christ in God.' I know, Neil. That's my problem. How do I do that?"

"Read it once again," I pressed, "just a little slower."

"'For you died—'" And suddenly a light switched on in his understanding. "Hey, that's past tense, isn't it?"

"Absolutely. Your problem is that

what Christ has already done for you."

Thanks to the incredible way God bought us out of sin through Christ's death on the cross, your old self is now replaced by a new self and controlled by a new nature. Second Corinthians 5:17 says, "Therefore, if anyone is in Christ, he is a new creation; the old has gone, the new has come!" When you received Christ, your old self died because Christ died, and your new self sprang to life because He was resurrected. First Corinthians 15:20-22 states, "But Christ has indeed been raised from the dead, the firstfruits of those who have fallen asleep. For since death came through a man, the resurrection of the dead comes also through a man. For as in Adam all die, so in Christ all will be made alive."

The new life which characterizes your new self is nothing less than the life of Jesus Christ implanted in you. Galatians 2:20 reminds us, "I have been crucified with Christ and I no longer live, but Christ lives in me. The life I live in the body, I live by faith in the Son of God, who loved me and gave himself for me." And Colossians 3:4 says, "When Christ, who is your life, appears, then you also will appear with him in glory."

Each of us must learn to base our behavior on our new master and on our new self which is joined with the nature of Christ. We must learn how to replace those old patterns of thinking that automatically respond to our sin-trained flesh. This transformation will take place as we renew our minds with the Word of God and walk in the Spirit.

Do you ever struggle because you feel like your old self hasn't died yet?

At what point did your old self die? (Reread Colossians 3:3 and Romans 6:6.)

THE LIE TO REJECT:

I reject the lie that I can overcome my past and live a righteous life by my own hard work and effort.

THE TRUTH TO ACCEPT:

I accept the truth that through Christ's death, burial, and resurrection my old self was put to death and was replaced by the life of Christ implanted in me. I am who I am by the grace of God.

PRAYER FOR TODAY:

Dear heavenly Father, You paid the debt for all my sins through the death of Jesus Your Son. Thank You for putting my old self to death and giving me new life in Christ. I know I can't do anything to become what You have already made me. There is not something You expect me to do in order for this to be true, it is something You expect me to believe. I choose to accept it and believe it. In Jesus' name I pray. Amen.

DAY TEN

...business. Instead, I have called you friends,
for everything that I learned from my Father I have
made known to you. You did not choose me, but I
chose you to go and bear fruit—fruit that will last.
Then the Father will give you whatever you ask in
my name. This is my command: Love each other
(John 15:12-17).

The world is often an unfriendly place. We can easily feel unloved, like nobody cares. But there is someone, a very significant someone who loves you. He has your best interests at heart. He'll stand by you in your lowest moments; He even sacrificed His life to meet your needs. Of course, we're talking about Jesus.

In Christ you have the best friend you could ever have. People may desert you during times of trouble, but Jesus invites you to draw near to Him. He takes you into His confidence: "Everything that I learned from my Father I have made known to you" (John 15:15). He also says, "When he, the Spirit of truth, comes, he will guide you into all truth. . . . All that belongs to the Father is mine. That is why I said the Spirit will take from what is mine and make it known to you" (John 16:13,15). Jesus discloses Himself to us . . .we know Him . . . He invites us to draw near. . . . He is the friend who sticks closer than a brother, the One who stays with us through all our tough times.

On one occasion I (Dave) was invited to speak in India. I love going to India, but after I arrived I got so sick I couldn't even walk and had to be carried into the hospital! It was a time when I truly needed a friend. I had food poisoning and the infection was so great that my temperature was 104. The dehydration was so bad that I had to receive six bottles of intervenous fluids! For three days I was in the hospital, only able to drink small amounts of water. I was hurting and alone. At times like that you really appreciate a visit from a friend. Larry Beckner travels with me, and he spent one night at the hospital with me. His presence and his prayers truly ministered to me.

But while Larry's presence meant so much, I sensed another presence that was even more comforting. I cried out to God and told Him how I felt. I was weak, tired, halfway around the world, and as far away from my wife and children as I could possibly be. I was lonely. Tears began to fill my eyes, not from pain and loneliness, but from peace. God's presence was right there in that hospital room. Jesus was comforting me. He was there the whole time. He is always with me and with you.

Jesus is the ultimate friend. He sacrificed Himself on the cross to meet our greatest need: "This is how we know what love is: Jesus Christ laid down his life for us" (1 John 3:16). He is your friend because *He chose to be your friend; He chose you.*

Have you ever wished that a certain person in your life would be your friend? Perhaps you thought, *I am going to do whatever I can to make him my friend,* only to be disappointed because he had his own agenda and didn't share your desire for friendship

I reject the lie that God is distant and that He is not my friend.

The Truth to Accept:

I accept the truth that Christ is my friend and that He chose me to be His friend.

Prayer for Today:

Dear heavenly Father, What a privilege it is to call You Father. How thankful I am that You have chosen me for Your friend. I renounce the lie that I am not worthy to be Your friend, because You have made me worthy. I renounce the lie that everybody is Your friend except me. And I announce the truth that I, too, am Your friend, because You have chosen me. From this day forward, I want to express my love to You by being open and honest about myself to You and by loving and being real with other people. Thank You for the privilege, thank You for the calling, thank You for choosing me. In Jesus' precious name I pray. Amen.

EXTREME EXTRAS

EXPLORE THE WORD

Write out what these verses say about you.

(Romans 8:17): _____

(1 Corinthians 3:16; 6:19):_____

(1 Corinthians 12:27): _____

(2 Corinthians 5:17-19):_____

(Galatians 3:26,28):_____

(Galatians 4:6,7):_____

(Ephesians 1:1; Philippians 1:1, Colossians 1:2): _____

EXPAND YOUR MIND

Memorize Galatians 4:6-7:

> Because you are sons, God sent the Spirit of
> his Son into our hearts, the Spirit who calls out,
> "Abba, Father." So you are no longer a slave,
> but a son; and since you are a son, God has
> made you also an heir.

father say "I love you" or "I'm glad you're my daughter." Her father was kind and loving at church and in front of other people, but at home it was, "Jamie, I'm too busy right now" or "Jamie, just leave me alone, can't you see I want to relax?" But Jamie's twin sister seemed to do no wrong; she was loved and accepted. "Why not me?" Jamie asked herself.

Then it happened—a terrible bike accident! The ambulance came roaring down the street. Jamie's head was scraped up and bleeding, and her clothes were torn and dirty. She was rushed to the hospital. Her anxious parents, brother, and sister were brought into the emergency room. "Jamie, are you all right, honey?" asked her mother. "Who are you?" asked Jamie. Her family was stunned; Jamie didn't recognize her own father or mother—not even her twin sister. The doctors ran test after test to try to determine why Jamie couldn't remember. The days slipped into weeks and still the doctors had no clue as to what had caused Jamie's mysterious memory loss. Jamie had to be reintroduced to her friends and had to relearn the simplest of tasks.

But Jamie was hiding a secret—a terrible secret. The truth was that Jamie was so desperate for her father's love that she faked amnesia! She had concocted the bike accident. She had even cut and scraped her own face to make the accident look real. For two years Jamie lived a lie.

Why did she do it? Why did she put her parents and family through so much pain? Because Jamie thought that if she could get a second chance to be someone else, then her father would love and accept her. She would be good this time—like her twin sister.

Jamie learned how hard it is to live a lie. She told me that it just got too complicated. She couldn't remember what lies she told and who she told them to. It was all too much to manage. And after two terrible years, her father was still ignoring her, and she felt as distant and unloved as before.

Finally, the lies and deceptions were too much for her to bear. She went to her mother and told her the truth. John 8:32 says, "Then you will know the truth, and the truth will set you free." As hard as it was for Jamie to tell the truth after two years of lies, she told me it felt good to have it out in the open. God loves it when we walk in the truth. Third John 4 says, "I have no greater joy than to hear that my children are walking in the truth." Jamie was deceived; she thought that if she was different or good enough, her father would love her. But you can never earn anyone's love; they either love you or they don't.

Jamie's picture of her earthly father and how he failed to accept and love her, carried over to her picture of God. Sometimes you might feel like Jamie. If you could just change—be good—then God would love you! Listen! You're His child. He already loves you! He proved that by sending Jesus to die for you. He has always loved you, and always will. Nothing you do will make Him love you more and nothing you can do will make Him love you less.

You probably know John

God is and how much He loves you!

Rich Miller, Director of Freedom in Christ Young Adult Ministries, and author of *To My Dear Slimeball*, has written a wonderful guide that will lead you to the truth about your heavenly Father. Begin each numbered phrase by reading out loud the bold section first.

The Truth About Our Heavenly Father

I renounce the lie that my heavenly Father is:

I joyfully accept the truth that my heavenly Father is:

1. distant and disinterested.
1. intimate and involved.

2. insensitive and uncaring.
2. kind and compassionate.

3. stern and demanding.
3. accepting and filled with joyful love.

4. passive and cold.
4. warm and affectionate.

5. absent or too busy for me.
5. always with me and always eager to spend time with me.

6. never satisfied with what I do, or that he is impatient or angry.
6. Patient, slow to anger, and pleased with me in Christ.

7. mean, cruel, or abusive.

7. loving, gentle, and protective of me.

8. trying to take all the joy and fun out of my life.

8. trustworthy. He wants to give me a full life; His will is good, perfect, and acceptable for me.

9. controlling or manipulative.

9. full of grace and mercy; He gives me freedom to live as I choose— even if I'm wrong.

10. condemning or unforgiving

10. tender-hearted and forgiving; and His heart and arms are always open to me.[1]

Remember, the truth you just announced about your heavenly Father is true even if you don't feel like it is. If the enemy puts thoughts in your head that are opposite from what you just proclaimed, tell him to get lost, and choose to believe the truth.

Say the following statements out loud:

THE LIE TO REJECT:

I reject the lie that God is uncaring or unloving.

THE TRUTH TO ACCEPT:

I accept the truth that God loves and cares for me so deeply that, to have a relationship with me, He sent His most precious Son to die for my sins.

love. I ask this in Jesus' name. Amen.

Day Twelve

Therefore, since we have been justified through faith, we have peace with God through our Lord Jesus Christ (Romans 5:1).

The school in the small farming town where I (Neil) was raised released students from school early every Tuesday afternoon for religious day instruction. Some of us went to the church of our choice for an hour of Bible study; those who chose not to go to church went to study hall. One Tuesday afternoon, a friend and I decided we would skip school and church this time, so we went and played in the gravel pit.

The next day the principal called me in and confronted me with the fact that I had skipped school. He concluded his remarks by saying he had arranged for me to stay home from school on Thursday and Friday of that week. I was shocked. No way! I was suspended from school for two days for skipping religious day instruction!

As I rode the school bus home that afternoon, I was terrified. I walked slowly up the long lane that led to our house, fearing my parents' wrath. I thought about faking an illness for two days or getting dressed for school as usual but hiding in the woods each day. . . . No, I couldn't do that to my parents. Lying wasn't the answer.

There was great unrest in my heart as I trudged up that lane. Because I was suspended from school, there was no way I could hide from my parents what I had done. When I finally told them, they were surprised, but then my mother started to smile. Without my knowing, she had called the principal earlier that week and asked permission for me to be released from school for two days to help with the fall harvest. I had already been justified for not going to school those two days!

Many young Christians fear the prospect of facing an angry God, knowing that He is holy and they are sinful. They can't grasp the fact that they are already justified. Their sins have already been taken care of by Jesus!

Romans 5:1 clearly says we *have already been justified* before a Holy Father. Jesus *has already paid* the penalty for our sins, establishing our peace with God the Father. When something has already been done, there is nothing left for you to do. Many believers try desperately to become something they already are, but the Bible declares that you cannot do for yourself what has already been done for you by Christ! The enemy's lie is that you must atone for your sin by works and, thereby, prove your love for God. The occult and non-Christian religions teach that.

To be righteous means to be brought perfectly in line with God's character and qualities of goodness and purity. But we know we're not born righteous. Romans 5:18 says, "Just as the result of one trespass was condemnation

3:22 tells us, "This righteousness from God comes through faith in Jesus Christ to all who believe." To believe means to put your trust in. "You have been set free from sin and have become slaves to righteousness" (Romans 6:18).

Faith is the only means by which you and I can enter into a relationship with God. Galatians 2:16 says, "Know that a man is not justified by observing the law, but by faith in Jesus Christ. So we, too, have put our faith in Christ Jesus that we may be justified by faith in Christ and not by observing the law, because by observing the law no one will be justified." I cannot do for myself what Christ alone could and has done for me.

The little preposition "in" plays a critical role in the New Testament. The fact that you are *in Christ*, that you are *in union* with Him, means that you are spiritually alive—you have *already been justified* before God.

What does that mean exactly? Look at Romans 5:9-11:

> Since we have now been justified by his blood, how much more shall we be saved from God's wrath through him! For if, when we were God's enemies, we were reconciled to him through the death of his Son, how much more, having been reconciled, shall we be saved through his life! Not only is this so, but

we also rejoice in God through our Lord Jesus Christ, through whom we have now received reconciliation.

Here are four results of our justification, as revealed in Romans 5:9-11.

First, we are saved from God's wrath; our future is secure because God's wrath is satisfied. You say, "Great, I have escaped eternal damnation." True, but there is *much more.* The *second* result of our justification is that we have peace with God. Before, we were His enemies; now, we are His friends. Facing God would be a total bummer if we were not already justified. When I ditched school that day, I was not looking forward to facing the judgment, rejection, or punishment of my parents. Knowing I was already justified and forgiven would have caused me to want to run to their loving arms rather than hanging back in dread and fear. We have peace with God. We don't have to pursue that peace—by the grace of God we have it now.

But that's not all! There's still *much more.* The *third* result of our justification is that we are saved through His life. My present life is already alive in Christ; I have spiritual life now. Eternal life is not something we receive when we die; we possess it now.

Well, is that it? No! The *fourth* and final result of our justification is that we also rejoice. John's stated purpose for his first epistle is, "We proclaim to you what we have seen and heard, so that you also may have fellowship with us. And our fellowship is with the Father and with his son, Jesus Christ. We write this to make our joy complete" (1 John 1:3,4). Many Christians are trying to appease an angry God to avoid punishment, when they could be pursuing a loving God whose justice was satisfied by the

How is a person justified? Check out Romans 10:10!

How does it feel to know you have been declared righteous in the sight of God because of the finished work of Jesus Christ? Write out your feelings!

Say the following statements out loud:

The Lie to Reject:

I reject the lie that I can in any way justify myself through any work or deed.

The Truth to Accept:

I accept the truth that I am completely justified through Christ's death, burial, and resurrection.

Prayer for Today:

Dear heavenly Father, I thank You for sending Your only begotten Son to pay the price in order that I may be justified. I now accept by faith that I have peace with You through my Lord Jesus Christ who took care of my sins for me. I renounce the lie that we are enemies, and claim the truth that we are friends, reconciled by the death of Your Son. I rejoice in the life that I now have in Christ, and I look forward to the day when I shall see You face to face. In Jesus' precious name I pray. Amen.

DAY THIRTEEN

God demonstrates His own love for us in this: While we were still sinners, Christ died for us (Romans 5:8).

The Bible uses a specific Greek term for God's love—*agape*. You have probably heard this word before. It means a self-sacrificing kind of love. God's love is what saved us from sin so we could spend eternity with Jesus in heaven. But being a Christian is more than just getting something; it's being someone. Jesus said, "I have come that they may have life, and have it to the full" (John 10:10). We receive more than a ticket to heaven when we accept Christ; we experience God's love, peace, and joy. Our personal relationship with God doesn't start when we get to heaven—it begins the moment we trust Christ. And God's love for us began long before we ever put our trust in Him. Romans 5:8 reminds us, "God demonstrates His own love for us in this: While we were still sinners, Christ died for us." God's great love for us moves us from the position of sinner to child of God. John 1:12 states "Yet to all who received him, to those who believed in his name, he gave the right to become children of God." I (Dave) wrote a prose-poem that expresses God's love and acceptance:

Love, as the world calls it, and God's love are two different things. The world's love is like the slow death of a starved old man, while God's love is like the joyful entrance of a newborn babe.

The world's love is as weak as a politician's promise, but God's love is as solid and strong as a granite peak that has been there for millenniums.

His love comforts. It's a soothing ointment that takes away the sting of a terrible burn, while the world's love leaves you wanting, like a half-cup of lukewarm soup.

God's love transforms a sin-sick heart into a saint, a child of the Most High God, while the world's makes you grope and grovel in the dark, searching for something it knows you cannot find.

The love of God transports you to heaven, where peace like a quiet stream fills your soul day after day, where joy and laughter ring like a child at Christmas.

The world's love follows you and tracks you down, to bind you and torment you. Its goal is destruction.

The world's love leads you to the gutter. Its words are death, cold like steel, unmerciful, unbending. There is no forgiveness there, only wicked shouts and accusations that cut like a dull knife through your very being.

But the love of God beckons you to come. It does not send you away, it is not hard to find. It calls out like a mother for a child. Like an angel that proclaims the glory of God, it never ceases. God calls out to you, "Come!" His voice echoes across all that is, "Yes you, come closer, deeper in. Sit upon My lap, let Me look at you. Let Me hold you My child, I love you. I love you. I will always love you."

God desperately wants to fellowship with us, to have us experience His love. Revelation 3:20, written to believers, gives us a beautiful picture of God's desire for fellowship with us: "Here I am! I stand at the door and knock. If anyone hears my voice and opens the door, I will come in and eat with him, and he with me." Sometimes we fail to experience God's love because we don't let Him into our lives; we resist His love. The world's love sometimes seems attractive to us, but, at its best, it still leaves us unfulfilled and wanting. Only God's love truly satisfies.

We don't often think of truth as being something we need, but truth is the key that unlocks the shackles of bondage. John 8:32 says, "Then you will know the truth, and the truth will set you free." We've heard it said that when you find a promise in the Bible, claim it; a command, obey it; and truth, believe it. That's good advice. But do you ever say to yourself, "I wish I could believe that" or "I'm sure that's true for others, but it's not true for me"?

Some people mistakenly think—or get deceived by the enemy into thinking—that the truth is difficult to shifting feelings. As the truth sinks inside, in time our feelings will change. Our world has lost its sense of God's absolutes (things that are always true). Truth is based on the person of Jesus Christ. Not only is what He says truth, but *He is truth*. Jesus said, "I am the way and the truth and the life" (John 14:6). Jesus identifies Himself as truth. Your believing that something is true doesn't make it true; it's true, therefore you believe it.

You may not feel like God loves you or that God is trustworthy. But God's Word tells us He is loving and He loves you. His Word shows us His trustworthiness, and you can believe His Word. So we must not look to our feelings, which we can't always control, but rather to the truth. We can always believe what God's Word tells us!

Say the following statements out loud:

THE LIE TO REJECT:

> I reject the lie that my feelings accurately measure God's love for me.

THE TRUTH TO ACCEPT:

> I accept the truth that God's Word reveals to me God's great love, and I choose to trust the truth, not my feelings.

PRAYER FOR TODAY:

Dear heavenly Father, I don't always feel loved. But Your Word tells me that You always love me. Help me to not look to my feelings, but rather to the truth. Lord, I know that I can't always control my feelings, but I can always believe what is true! I choose to believe the truth that I am loved. In Jesus' name I pray. Amen.

DAY FOURTEEN

If we confess our sins, he is faithful and just and will forgive us our sins and purify us from all unrighteousness (1 John 1:9).

The Christian walk is a life of progress not perfection. God wants us to model growth. He knows that, as humans, we can't model perfection. When you sin you don't become a sinner again; you're in Christ and nothing can change that. You may sometimes feel like, once you blow it, God won't forgive you or take you back into fellowship with Him. Some say, "I had my shot at freedom and I blew it." But God never stops loving us or forgiving us. He never gives up on us. He always accepts us.

Floyd McCung, Jr., in his book *The Father Heart of God* tells a great story about a father's unconditional love for his son.

Sawat had disgraced his family and dishonored his father's name. He had come to Bangkok to escape the dullness of village life. He had found

That visit began Sawat's venture into Bangkok's world of prostitution. It began innocently enough, but he was quickly caught like a small piece of wood in a raging river. Its force too powerful and swift for him, the current too strong.

Soon he was selling opium to customers and propositioning tourists in the hotels. He even went so low as to actually help buy and sell young girls, some of them only nine and ten years old. It was a nasty business, and he was one of the most important of the young "businessmen."

Then the bottom dropped out of his world: He hit a string of bad luck. He was robbed, and while trying to climb back to the top, he was arrested. The word went out in the underworld that he was a police spy. He finally ended up living in a shanty by the city trash pile.

Sitting in his little shack, he thought about his family, especially his father, a simple Christian man from a small southern village near the Malaysian border. He remembered his dad's parting words: "I am waiting for you." He wondered whether his father would still be waiting for him after all that he had done to dishonor the family name. Would he be welcome in his home? Word of Sawat's lifestyle had long ago filtered back to the village.

Finally he devised a plan.

"Dear Father," he wrote, "I wanted to come home, but I don't know if you will receive me after all that I have done. I have sinned greatly, Father. Please forgive me. On Saturday night I will be on the train that goes through our village. If you are still waiting for me, will you tie a piece of cloth on the po tree in front of our house? (signed) Sawat."

On that train ride he reflected on his life over the past few months and knew that his father had every right to deny him. As the train finally neared the village, he churned with anxiety. What would he do if there was no white cloth on the po tree?

Sitting opposite him was a kind stranger who noticed how nervous his fellow passenger had become. Finally Sawat could stand the pressure no longer. He blurted out his story in a torrent of words. As they entered the village, Sawat said, "Oh, sir, I cannot bear to look. Can you watch for me? What if my father will not receive me back?"

Sawat buried his face between his knees. "Do you see it, sir? It's the only house with a po tree."

"Young man, your father did not hang just one piece of cloth. Look! He has covered the whole tree with cloth!" Sawat could hardly believe his eyes. The branches were laden with tiny white squares. In the front yard his old father jumped up and down, joyously waving a piece of white cloth, then ran in halting steps beside the train. When it stopped at the little station he threw his arms around his son, always be true. We can't overuse them or wear them out. At no time will God ever give up on you. He will never leave you, never forsake you. Jesus tells us, "Surely I am with you always, to the very end of the age" (Matthew 28:20).

THE LIE TO REJECT:

I reject the lie that God will not forgive me or cleanse me from my sin.

THE TRUTH TO ACCEPT:

I accept the truth that if I agree with God that I have sinned, and confess it to Him, He will always forgive and cleanse me.

PRAYER FOR TODAY:

Dear heavenly Father, Thank You that I can always come to You, that You are faithful and righteous and always willing to forgive. Help me recognize when I sin and be quick to admit, confess, and renounce it to You and seek Your forgiveness. I want to be an example to those around me, so cleanse me from my sin and let Your righteousness shine through me. In Jesus' name I pray. Amen.

DAY FIFTEEN

He predestined us to be adopted as his sons through Jesus Christ, in accordance with his pleasure and will (Ephesians 1:5).

In the middle of the last century, out on the plains of Nebraska, a circuit preacher made his rounds from church to church and from town to town. In one community, he found a little orphan boy, an immigrant named Peter Popavich. Peter's family had been killed in one of the range wars that had taken its toll on many people. Peter was incorrigible and a troublemaker, causing others to shun him.

Because none of the townsfolk would take him into their homes, the preacher assumed Peter as his responsibility. He took the little boy wherever he went, but soon realized this could not continue. Then he heard of a Christian couple, Mr. and Mrs. Smith, who had a boy named Sammy, about the same age as Peter. The circuit preacher rode out to their farm and asked the Smiths if they would consider raising Peter. They prayed about it and agreed together as a family that this was God's will for their lives, so they took on the responsibility.

The chemistry of relationships is an interesting thing. Sammy was a loving, supportive little boy, while Peter remained his old trouble-making self. Regardless, the two boys became the best of friends. One day they were playing together near a slough that was quarantined because of contamination. A sign clearly announced the danger. Peter said, "Let's go swimming." But Sammy refused. Peter said, "Well, I'm going." And in he went. He cut his foot on the surrounding barbed wire fence, and it gone, the desire of the two boys to be together again was overwhelming, and when the parents returned home they found the boys asleep in each other's arms. Nobody fully understands the providential nature of God; Peter got well, but Sammy got sick. Within days, Sammy died.

Several years passed, and the circuit preacher again happened to be making his rounds in that same community. He remembered Peter and decided to stop to see how he was. As he rode up to the farm, he recognized Mr. Smith, but he didn't recognize the big, strong, strapping boy standing beside him. "What happened to the boy I dropped by here several years ago?" the preacher asked.

Mr. Smith reached up and put his arm around the boy. "This is Peter Smith," he said. "We have adopted him as part of our family."

Before he was adopted, Peter was without a family. The Smiths didn't *need* Peter, but they *wanted* him. Peter could let go of the rejection he felt in the past and accept the love of the father who chose to adopt him. Our heavenly Father doesn't *need* us, but He *wants* us. This unconditional love and acceptance of God is the essential foundation for holy living.

"But you are a chosen people, a royal priesthood, a holy nation, a people belonging to God, that you may declare the praises of him who called you out of darkness into his wonderful light. Once you were not a people, but now you are the people of God; once you had not received mercy, but now you have received mercy" (1 Peter 2:9,10). God has no throwaway children; none of us are unwanted or unexpected accidents. "He chose us in him, before the creation of the world to be holy and blameless in his sight" (Ephesians 1:4).

One of Satan's most common lies is that somehow you and I are different from other people. We may think, *God accepts these other people but not me.* But we don't have to be afraid of losing God's love. Titus 3:4,5 tells us, "But when the kindness and love of God our Savior appeared, he saved us, not because of righteous things we had done, but because of his mercy." Where once we had not received mercy, now we have. "Consequently, you are no longer foreigners and aliens, but fellow citizens with God's people and members of God's household" (Ephesians 2:19).

THE LIE TO REJECT:

I reject the lie that I am a stranger to God and that He has rejected me.

THE TRUTH TO ACCEPT:

I accept the truth that God chose me, accepts me, and loves me unconditionally.

PRAYER FOR TODAY:

Dear heavenly Father, Thank You for loving and choosing me. I reject the lies of Satan that You don't want me or care for me. I choose to believe that I am no longer a stranger to You.

EXTREME EXTRAS

EXPLORE THE WORD

Write out what these verses say about you.

(Ephesians 2:19): _____

(Ephesians 3:1; 4:1): _____

(Ephesians 4:24): _____

(Ephesians 2:6; Philippians 3:20): _____

(Colossians 3:3,4): _____

(Colossians 3:12; 1 Thessalonians 1:4): _____

(1 Thessalonians 5:5): _____

(Hebrews 3:1): _____

(Hebrews 3:14): _____

EXPAND YOUR MIND

Memorize 1 Thessalonians 5:5:

You are all sons of the light and sons of the day. We do not belong to the night or to the darkness.

EXPRESS YOURSELF

_____

_____

_____

_____

_____

_____

_____

_____

_____

_____

_____

_____

_____

_____

1

LEARNING TO TRUST GOD

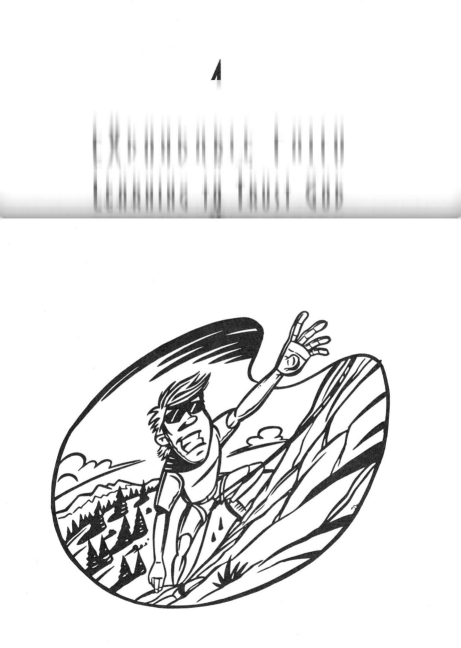

ply doesn't care? You see God help others in their time of need and wonder why He doesn't help you.

That's exactly how Kay felt. Kay came to me (Dave) to get help for some nightmares she was having. Her dreams involved the murder of her family members. In one of them, Kay found herself on a beautiful lakeside where she was fishing with her friends and family. The sky was blue, the air fresh and clear. Suddenly she felt a tug on the line. She had one. She began to reel her line in, faster and faster. As her catch neared the shore, she looked down in horror—at the end of her line was the drowned body of her mother.

I asked Kay if she could remember a traumatic event in her life that might be causing these awful nightmares. The enemy is cruel and will even place murderous thoughts in our dreams to confuse and hurt us. "Well . . ." Kay paused, and without much expression, she said, "I was raped." Kay had been enjoying a trip overseas, when she found herself alone with a guy she thought she could trust—but he brutally raped her. During the attack, she cried out to God continually in her mind, "Lord, please help me! Don't let this happen to me! Rescue me, please rescue me!" But it didn't stop. Kay felt herself sink away, as if she weren't there. To this day she still can't recall all that happened that terrible day.

Kay stared at me, her eyes filled with tears. "Why didn't God help me?" she asked. "Why in my time of need did God bail out on me? Doesn't He love me?"

I felt compelled to simply sit quietly for a moment, sharing in her grief. After a time, I asked Kay if she could think of any act of God that proved His love for her.

"Yeah," she mumbled, "Jesus died on the cross."

"Kay, I know you understand the 'fact' that Christ died for you, but I wonder if you realize that His death for you was an act of rescue! No one can explain the terrible rape that you were forced to endure, or why that man chose to hurt you the way he did. But we can go to a specific point in time—the death of Christ—and see how God loved you so much that He was willing to die to rescue you. Can you trust a God who would do that for you?"

Kay had already gone through the *Steps to Freedom*, biblical principles that deal with the most common areas in which Satan is likely to deceive us, so I encouraged her to ask God to reveal to her whether or not she had forgiven the man who violated her and if she had accepted forgiveness for the thoughts against God that she might have had.

Five days later she called to tell me that the nightmares had stopped, and she was walking free. We can't promise you that something terrible won't happen to you some day because we live in a sick and fallen world. But we can say that, in Christ, you can find resolution and be free of the pain in your past.

The truth is, God never did forsake Kay or fail her. Psalm 9:10 tells us, "Those who know your name will trust in you, for you, LORD, have never forsaken those who seek you." God has an unfailing love for Kay, and even when terrible, unspeakable things happen in her

Satan or one of his cohorts may know the events of your life, as well. The enemy tries at every turn to twist what happens in your life; he creates lies in your mind that oppose God's truth. That's why we must look to the truth and not to our feelings. Talk to God about what you're feeling, but also announce out loud the truth of what His Word says. Take time to be still and let God speak to you. If you have trouble thinking or concentrating on God, tell the enemy, out loud, to get.

Say the following statements out loud:

The Lie to Reject:

I reject the lie that God will forsake or fail me.

The Truth to Accept:

I accept the truth that God cares for me and that His love for me is unfailing.

Prayer for Today:

Dear heavenly Father, Thank You for Your unfailing love. I choose to trust in You with all my heart and lean not on my own understanding. I know, Father, that sometimes I have unbiblical expectations of You. I know You are perfect and pure. You cannot change to conform to my expectations, and I'm glad You don't. I know You will never forsake me because Your Word tells me You won't. Thank You for always being here with me. Thank You for Your unfailing love. In Jesus' name I pray. Amen.

DAY SEVENTEEN

Who shall separate us from the love of Christ? Shall trouble or hardship or persecution or famine or nakedness or danger or sword? As it is written: "For your sake we face death all day long; we are considered as sheep to be slaughtered." No, in all these things we are more than conquerors through him who loved us. For I am convinced that neither death nor life, neither angels nor demons, neither the present nor the future, nor any powers, neither height nor depth, nor anything else in all creation, will be able to separate us from the love of God that is in Christ Jesus our Lord (Romans 8:35-39).

The core issue of security is relationship. There is no greater assurance than that which is found in relationships built on trust and commitment. Likewise, there is no greater insecurity than when a significant relationship is threatened by desertion, danger, or destruction.

Both Dave and I live in Colorado. Once, while driving in the mountains with my wife, I happened upon an elk herd crossing the road. They leaped a barbed-wire the security of the herd, and every animal felt the pain. Thankfully, the baby elk eventually made it safely through the fence.

What must it be like to have hardships so severe that a parent must leave home to find work or the children must be split up among friends and relatives for their survival? One can hardly imagine the turmoil of families torn apart because of persecution or the tremendous pain felt during the time of slavery when mothers and fathers and children were sold separately. Many of you who are reading this know the pain of experiencing your parents' divorce.

Paul wrote of hard times like these under the inspiration of God, but also from the experiences of his own life:

> Five times I received from the Jews the forty lashes minus one. Three times I was beaten with rods, once I was stoned, three times I was shipwrecked, I spent a night and a day in the open sea, I have been constantly on the move. I have been in danger from rivers, in danger from bandits, in danger from my own countrymen, in danger from Gentiles; in danger in the city, in danger in the country, in danger at sea; and in danger from false brothers. I have labored and toiled and have often gone without sleep; I have known hunger and thirst

and have often gone without food; I have been cold and naked. Besides everything else, I face daily the pressure of my concern for all the churches. Who is weak, and I do not feel weak? Who is led into sin, and I do not inwardly burn? (2 Corinthians 11:24-29).

Did Paul's hardships separate him from the love of God? No, nothing the world can throw at us can interfere with the eternal security we have in Christ. God's love was still at work in Paul's life and certainly in the lives of those whom Paul wanted to reach for Christ. Paul addresses this when he quotes from Psalm 44:22: "For your sake we face death all day long; we are considered as sheep to be slaughtered" (Romans 8:36).

God's chosen people often have to face difficult trials and tribulations for His work to be accomplished. We will experience suffering in this lifetime. So we need to adopt the attitude of the early church, when the Sanhedrin (the ruling religious leaders of that time) rejected and beat Christians for proclaiming Christ. Acts 5:41 says, "The apostles left the Sanhedrin, rejoicing because they had been counted worthy of suffering disgrace for the Name." Then Paul writes in 2 Timothy 3:12, "In fact, everyone who wants to live a godly life in Christ Jesus will be persecuted."

Paul exclaimed that in all of these things we are more than conquerors through Him who loves us. But some may say, "So, because of our relationship with God we have an eternal relationship that cannot be overcome by the temporary problems of life, but what about the supernatural issues? What about uncontrollable things that are looming ahead?" Paul's answer: "I am convinced that neither death nor life, neither angels nor demons, neither the present nor the future, nor any powers, neither height nor depth, nor anything else in all creation, will be able to separate us from the love of God that is in Christ Jesus our Lord" (Romans 8:38,39).

Who has the power over life and death? Who has authority over the angelic realm? Who sovereignly governs the affairs of men and angels now and forever? Our heavenly Father is the Lord of eternity! We need not fear tomorrow, death, demons, or eternity. The shepherd of our souls says, "My sheep listen to my voice; I know them, and they follow me. I give them eternal life, and they shall never perish; no one can snatch them out of my hand. My Father, who has given them to me, is greater than all; no one can snatch them out of my Father's hand" (John 10:27-29). Our relationship with God is not a question of our ability to hang on to Him. That really isn't within our personal power to do anyway. The fact is, God holds on to us, and He has the power to keep us securely and safely in His hand.

The love of God surpasses knowledge—we can't fully comprehend how much He loves us. The skeptic may ask, "If God loves me, why does He allow so much persecution and hardship?" But we are left on earth for a purpose, and suffering for righteousness' sake is actually a privilege. In the midst of life's harsh realities, we can share with others that our security is not found in the temporal things of life but in the eternal relationship we have with our heavenly Father. Nothing in all creation can separate us from the love of God that is in Christ Jesus, our Lord.

Are you struggling through some temporary problems of life? Explain.

Are you having difficulty fully understanding the nature of God's eternal relationship and love for you? Explain.

Say the following statements out loud:

THE LIE TO REJECT:

I reject the lie that anything can separate me from the love of God.

THE TRUTH TO ACCEPT:

I accept the truth that neither death nor life, neither angels nor demons, neither the present nor the future, nor any power, neither height nor depth, nor anything else in all creation can separate me from the love of Jesus my Lord.

PRAYER FOR TODAY:

Dear heavenly Father, I pray that I may have power together with all the saints to grasp how wide and long and high and deep Your love is and to know this love that surpasses knowledge, so that I may be filled to the very top of my being with the fullness of God. In Jesus' precious name I pray. Amen.

DAY EIGHTEEN

Faith comes from hearing the message, and the message is heard through the word of Christ (Romans 10:17).

One Easter I (Dave) found myself on the road, so I called home to talk to my son David, who at that time was only three years old. I said, "Davers, it's Easter. Do you know what Easter is all about?"

"Yeah Daddy" he replied. "It's when Jesus died on the cross, but got all better because He's sooo God!"

That may be bad grammar, but it's great theology. What does it mean to be "sooo God?" How do we come to understand all that God is? Only through His Word, the Bible.

It is impossible for us to grow in our faith or trust in Christ apart from His Word. Romans 10:17 says, "Faith comes from hearing the message, and the message is heard through the Word of Christ." If you say, "I wish I could trust God," you're either deceived or still need to know what God's Word says. His Word shows us time and time again that He can be trusted. Hear the words of Jesus: "Do not let your hearts be troubled. Trust in God; trust also in me" (John 14:1). You may say, "But how do we know that what Jesus said is true?" The answer is found in the resurrection. The fact that Jesus overcame sin and death proved that He was God and, therefore, He's trustworthy. A lot of people in our lives fail us, but God never will.

Rock climbing isn't something I do a lot of, but on a few occasions I've found myself suspended from a rope, usually rappelling. Rappelling is a real act of trust; you have to trust the rope, the rock the rope is anchored to, and the person who is on the ground spotting you. If you fall, the spotter simply pulls the rope and you stop instantly. First-time rappellers usually are instructed to fall on purpose so they can experience the security of a trustworthy rope, spotter, and anchor. If you never fall, you will never know that the objects of your faith can be trusted. God is like that. He sometimes lets us fall so He can catch us. Isaiah 26:4 says, "Trust in the LORD forever, for the LORD, the LORD, is the Rock eternal."

Remember Kay from Day Sixteen? She found several events in her life that made it look as though God had forgotten her and failed to rescue her. Yet, after checking out God's Word, she could clearly see that she had been tricked, deceived by the evil one. It was amazing to see her hope and joy return as she began to walk in the truth. "May the God of hope fill you with all joy and peace as you trust in him, so that you may overflow with hope by the power of the Holy Spirit" (Romans 15:13). This verse describes Kay; does it describe you?

God's Word reveals His qualities, and those qualities prove His trustworthiness.

If God were to appear on the Dave Letterman show, what would be His top ten qualities? Picture it. Dave would glare at the camera with his split buck teeth and say, "Let's look at *God's Top 10 Qualities*, the ones that prove He can be trusted."

GOD'S TOP 10 QUALITIES

10. God doesn't need to ask for permission. He's the chief, head honcho, numero uno, boss, ruler, president, CEO of all that is. God has complete control.

9. God doesn't die, pass away, kick the bucket, get knocked off, or rubbed out. He's the eternal one, outlasting the EverReady bunny. He's not bound to time. He's always been around. He sees the past, present, and future. He's got no beginning and no end. He is eternal.

8. God doesn't need help when He watches "Jeopardy"; He knows all the answers. He knows all the questions. Nothing surprises Him. He created knowledge and has all knowledge. God knows everything.

7. God doesn't need to travel to get there. He is already there, always has been there, always will be there. You can run, but you can't hide. He sees you; He never has His eyes off you. He fills all space. God is everywhere.

6. God doesn't need to recharge His batteries. He doesn't get tired, doesn't have to sit down, doesn't need a rest. He has total strength, never lacks strength. He can do all things at once and still use hardly any energy. His strength has no end, no limits. God is all powerful.

5. God doesn't say, "Oops, I didn't mean to do that." He never changes His mind. He doesn't flip-flop, doesn't have to rethink the issues. He always does

what He says He will do, keeps His Word. He keeps His promises. He's the same every day, always the same. The same yesterday, the same today, the same forever. God never changes.

4. God doesn't have to say, "Forgive Me, sorry, oh was that your foot?" He never made things go wrong, blew it, botched up, sinned, messed up. He never got a ticket, broke a law, was in any way incorrect. He's perfect. God is righteous.

3. God doesn't have to appeal to a higher court for justice; He is justice. He never treats anybody unfairly, never shows favoritism, never picks one over the other. He always shows mercy, always brings total justice. He's fair, unbiased. God is just.

2. God doesn't lie. He never told a little white lie, half truth, fib. He never stretched the truth, exaggerated, was confused, mistaken, or had the facts wrong. He's not a deceiver. He doesn't trick you or pull practical jokes. He doesn't try to confuse you, lead you astray, pull the wool over your eyes. He's always honest. If He says it's true, bank on it. God is total truth.

1. God doesn't wait until you get your act together to love you. He loves you if you have pimples, if you're overweight, if you're skinny, if you think you're smart, if you think you're dumb, if you brush your teeth, if you have no teeth, if you kick your dog. (Don't kick the dog!) He loves you even when you sin, loved you while you were still sinning, loved you when you didn't even know He loved you. His love is pure. His love is perfect. It never fails, never goes away, isn't conditional. He gives it

freely, doesn't hold back, pours it on, keeps it coming. God is love.

God is trustworthy because He is God. He doesn't conform to a standard—He is the standard. He is holy because holiness is defined by who God is. He is the fullness of purity and righteousness.

As you read about God's qualities did you feel your trust in Him grow?

The Lie to Reject:

I reject the lie that God is anything less than pure and perfect and that He cannot be trusted.

The Truth to Accept:

I accept the truth that God has been and always will be pure and perfect and trustworthy.

Prayer for Today:

Dear heavenly Father, Your awesome attributes are clearly seen in the world and in Your Word. I know that You are holy, pure, and perfect. But most of all, I thank You for Your incredible love—a love that reached out to me even when I was unlovely and not searching for You. You lovingly and patiently drew me to an understanding of who You are, so that I could put my trust in Christ. Lord, I want to learn more about You, to understand the depths of Your attributes and love. Help me to see You as You really are. In Jesus' name I pray. Amen.

DAY NINETEEN

Without faith it is impossible to please God, because anyone who comes to him must believe that he exists and that he rewards those who earnestly seek him (Hebrews 11:6).

What is faith? Second Corinthians 5:7 reminds us that "we live by faith, not by sight." The Christian life is a walk of faith; faith is the means by which we are saved. "For it is by grace you have been saved, through faith—and this not from yourselves, it is the gift of God—not by works, so that no one can boast (Ephesians 2:8,9). But what exactly is faith? We know we need faith to grow, for Colossians 2:6,7 says," . . . continue to live in him, rooted and built up in him, strengthened in the faith as you were taught, and overflowing with thankfulness." But that still doesn't tell us exactly what faith is. It is crucial that every believer live by faith, but many believers don't really know what faith is! Take a minute to put into your own words what faith means to you.

Did your definition include words like belief, trust, or dependence? Biblical faith is believing and trusting in Christ, depending on Him. Hebrews 11:6 tells us, "And without faith it is impossible to please God, because anyone who comes to him must believe that he exists and that he rewards those who earnestly seek him." Biblical faith requires an object. Charles Swindoll tells a story that illustrates the importance of having a trustworthy object of your faith.

A recent "Alfred Hitchcock" TV episode showed the flip-side to this sure and certain hope. As you might expect, the point was made in a rather chilling way.

There was this rather wicked, two-faced woman who murdered an individual. And though she had often done wrong on previous occasions and had always gotten away with it, the court found her guilty in this case, and the judge sentenced her to life in prison. Even though she screamed in the judge's face and announced that she would escape from any prison they put her into, they sent her away.

She took that infamous bus ride to the prison. Enroute, she noticed something that became part of her escape plan. She saw an old man, an inmate, covering up a grave outside the prison walls. She realized the only way to get out of the prison was to know someone who had the key to the gate. The only one who did was the old man who assisted in the burial of those who died within the walls. Actually, he built the caskets as well as placed the remains in each casket. His job included rolling the casket on an old cart to the gravesites outside the wall and then lowering it into the hole and covering it up with dirt.

The old man was going blind. He needed cataract surgery, but he had no money to pay for it. She told him it would be worth his while if he would help her escape.

"No ma'am, I can't do that."

"Oh, yes you can," she insisted. "I have all the money you need outside these walls to pay for your cataract surgery. And if you hope to have that operation, then you help me out of this place."

He reluctantly agreed.

Here was the plan: The next time she heard the toll of the bell, which signaled the death of an inmate, she would slip down to his workroom where he made the caskets. She was to locate the casket and pull the top down tightly. Early the next morning the old man would roll her, along with the corpse in the casket, out to the place of burial, drop it into the hole, and dump the dirt on it. The next day he was to come back, uncover the grave, pry the top loose, and set her free. Perfect plan. Almost.

Late one night she heard the deep toll of the bell . . . someone had died. This was her moment! She secretly slid off her cot, made her way down an eerie hallway, and, looking into the dimly lit room, she saw the casket. Without hesitation, she lifted the lid and slipped into the dark box and, after squeezing in beside the corpse, she pulled the lid down tightly.

Within a matter of hours she could feel the wheels rolling as they made their way to the gravesite. She smiled as the casket was placed in the hole. She heard the clumps of dirt hit the top of the casket. Before long, she was sealed beneath the earth—still smiling.

Silence followed. She could hardly contain her excitement. Time began to drag. The next day came and passed into the night without the old man showing up. By now she had broken into a cold sweat. Where was he? What could possibly have gone wrong? Why hadn't he shown up?

In a moment of panic she lit a match and glanced at the corpse next to her. You guessed it—it was the old man himself who had died!

Slowly, the camera lifted from the gravesite, and all you could hear was the hollow, wailing cry of the woman who would never get out of the grave.[1]

Everyone lives by faith. We all put our trust in something or someone. The main difference between the Christian and the non-Christian is the object of faith. Jesus is the only trustworthy object of faith because He is the only one that is unchanging: "Jesus Christ is the same yesterday and today and forever" (Hebrews 13:8). Any other object will eventually let you down. Only Jesus can be totally trusted.

THE LIE TO REJECT:

I reject the lie that there is any trustworthy object of my faith apart from Jesus Christ.

THE TRUTH TO ACCEPT:

I accept the truth that Jesus, who died at Calvary and rose again, is the only trustworthy object of my faith.

PRAYER FOR TODAY:

Dear heavenly Father, I put all my trust in You. The fact that Jesus died and rose from the dead proved that He truly was who He said He was, the Son of God. Lord, You are the only trustworthy object of my faith. I know you have given me a measure of faith so I choose to walk by faith and not by sight. In Jesus' name I pray. Amen.

DAY TWENTY

I have learned to be content whatever the circumstances. I know what it is to be in need, and I know what it is to have plenty. I have learned the secret of being content in any and every situation, whether well fed or hungry, whether living in plenty or in want. I can do everything through him who gives me strength (Philippians 4:11-13).

If God wants it done, can it be done? Does the Bible say, "With God *most* things are possible?" No, it says, "Everything is possible for him who believes" (Mark 9:23). If God tells us to do something, can we do it? God doesn't issue a command that cannot be carried out. That would be like Him saying, "Child, I want you to do something you won't be able to do, but give it your best shot anyway!" That's ludicrous!

So, what is the "everything" that we can do? Certainly there are some limitations. The key, as in all biblical interpretation, is found in the context. Paul says he has learned to be content in all of life's situations. In other words, the circumstances of life do not determine who we are, nor do they keep us from being what God wants us to be. No person and no circumstance can keep us from doing the will of God, because it is Christ who strengthens us (see Philippians 4:11-13).

We may not be able to rearrange the external events of life, nor have we been called to, but we have the assurance that God is using that external world to rearrange our *internal* world. "We also rejoice in our sufferings, because we know that suffering produces perseverance; perseverance, character; and character, hope.

And hope does not disappoint us, because God has poured out his love into our hearts by the Holy Spirit, whom he has given us" (Romans 5:3-5). Our hope lies in proven character, not in favorable circumstances, and that is where Paul learned the secret of contentment. He stopped trying to change the world and allowed God to change him. If we all did that, the world would be radically different.

The fruit of the Spirit isn't the ability to control either people or circumstances. The fruit of the Spirit is self-control. When we turn the control of our lives over to God, we move significantly closer to doing all things through Christ, stop trying to control our friends, and start showing them the love of Christ. Our unbelief is the only obstacle keeping us from first being and then doing all God wants us to be and do. We are assured in Mark 9:23 that all things are possible for those who believe. However, we can't determine for ourselves what it is we want to believe. We must believe the truth as it's found in God's Word.

New Age philosophers say, "If you believe something enough, it will become true." They argue that we can create reality with our minds. But in order to do that, we would have to be gods, which is precisely what they are saying. That lie goes all the way back to the garden . . . "You will be like God" (Genesis 3:5). At our youth conferences I (Dave) like to illustrate just how ridiculous this kind of thinking is by standing in front of the audience and imagining my body transformed to the shape and size of Arnold Schwarzenegger. After a few seconds I ask the audience, "Is it working?" After they finish laughing, they shout, "No" in perfect unison. No matter how long and hard I concentrate on having the body of Arnold Schwarzenegger, I'll never get it.

Christianity, on the other hand, says, "It is true, therefore I believe it." Believing something doesn't make it true, and not believing something doesn't cause it to go away. Jesus prayed for us concerning this: "My prayer is not that you take them out of the world but that you protect them from the evil one. . . . Sanctify them by the truth; your word is truth" (John 17:15,17). We believe in God and walk by faith according to His Word. In our book *Stomping Out the Darkness* we put it this way:

If You Believe You Can, You Can

If you think you are beaten, you are.
If you think you dare not, you don't.
If you want to win but think you can't,
It is almost a cinch you won't.
If you think you'll lose, you're lost.
For out of the world we find
That success begins with a fellow's will;
It's all in the state of mind.
Life's battles don't always go
To the stronger or the faster man;
But sooner or later the man that wins
Is the one who thinks he can. [2]

The Christian has a far greater potential in the power of believing the truth. Belief incorporates the mind, but is not limited by it. I may not understand a lot of biblical truth, but I still believe it. Belief, or faith, actually goes beyond the limitations of the mind and incorporates the world that is unseen but not unreal. With the infinite God of the universe as the object of Christian faith, what can stop the Christian if God wants something done? Also, it doesn't take any more effort to believe that one *can* than to believe that one *cannot*. The goal is to choose truth, to take every thought captive to the obedience of Christ, instead of believing the enemy's lies. Because you are God's child, you can confront doubts and unbelief.

We asked earlier, "If God wants it done, can it be done?" and "If God tells us to do something, can we do it?" The answer is, "Absolutely!" And if God gives you grace, can you be content with His will in any situation? Yes, because He is with you and you are in Him. You can say, "I can do everything through Him who gives me strength" (Philippians 4:13).

THE LIE TO REJECT:

I reject the lie of Satan that says I can't do what God asks of me.

THE TRUTH TO ACCEPT:

I accept the truth that I can do all things through Christ who strengthens me.

PRAYER FOR TODAY:

Dear heavenly Father, thank You for revealing my true identity in Christ. Thank You for showing me from Your Word how You are meeting my needs of acceptance, security, and significance in Christ. I feel like I need to say, "Lord, I believe, but help me in my unbelief." Teach me to take every thought captive to the obedience of Christ. I want to be a child of God who lives by faith. I renounce the lies of Satan that say I can't, and I announce the truth that I can do all things through Christ who strengthens me. I pray for the renewing of my mind so that I can prove that the will of God is good, acceptable, and perfect for me. I love You with all my heart, soul, and strength. You are the Lord of the universe, and the Lord of my life, now and forever. In Jesus' precious name I pray. Amen.

EXTREME EXTRAS

EXPLORE THE WORD

Write out what these verses say about you.

(1 Corinthians 15:10): _____

(1 Peter 2:5): _____

(1 Peter 2:11): _____

(1 Peter 5:8): _____

(1 John 3:1,2): _____

(1 John 5:18): _____

EXPAND YOUR MIND

Memorize 1 Peter 2:5:

You also, like living stones, are being built into a spiritual house to be a holy priesthood, offering spiritual sacrifices acceptable to God through Jesus Christ.

EXPRESS YOURSELF

5

X-Files on Fear
The Battle for the Mind

> *Be self-controlled and alert. Your enemy the devil prowls around like a roaring lion looking for someone to devour. Resist him, standing firm in the faith, because you know that your brothers throughout the world are undergoing the same kind of sufferings. And the God of all grace, who called you to his eternal glory in Christ, after you have suffered a little while, will himself restore you and make you strong, firm and steadfast (1 Peter 5:8-10).*

Some years ago I (Dave) had the opportunity to travel to Zaire, Africa, with several students on a missions trip. We had been working hard, so we decided to take a day off one weekend and head to Rwindi, a game preserve filled with exotic wildlife. Sight-seeing and fishing were just what we needed to relax and recharge our batteries.

We had barely entered the park when we happened upon two male lions fighting in the middle of the road. Undoubtedly they were fighting over a female; males are always trying to prove themselves! The local missionary who had lived there for close to 30 years began to explain to us the behavior of wild lions.

The male lions sleep about 18 hours a day. What bums! And the females do all of the hunting. To top it off, the females bring their catch to the male and he gets to eat first. What a life! Let me remind my male readers— God didn't create you to act like an animal.

The male lion does have one important role when it comes to hunting. His job is to go out into the savanna and begin to roar, while the ladies stay carefully hidden in the tall grass across from him. Stuck in the middle is the prey. The prey usually panics at the sound of the male lion's mighty roar and hightails it out of there—directly toward the female lions who are waiting to eat them for lunch.

The prey doesn't realize that the male lion is usually so big and lazy that he's not about to try to run down anything. His roar is an empty roar. What would happen if the prey didn't panic and just stood firm? They would avoid the trap that leads to death.

First Peter 5:8 reminds us to "be self-controlled and alert. Your enemy the devil prowls around like a *roaring lion* looking for someone to devour" (emphasis added). Peter uses the illustration of a lion because the devil, like the fat male lion, has certain limitations. Satan can't do one thing about who you are in Christ; he can't touch your position in Christ. But Satan is a good bluffer. He has a loud roar! Resist him, standing firm in the faith (1 Peter 5:9), and he can't harm you.

Satan is a master at creating fear, but nowhere in the Bible does it tell us to fear Satan and his host of fallen angels. Fear is created when something is powerful and present. To conquer fear from the enemy we need to simply understand that nothing is more powerful and present than God.

When you find freedom in Christ, you can sense God's presence and power. You can hear God's voice and understand the Bible; you can pray and worship Him. Those people caught in spiritual conflicts sometimes find it next to impossible to enter into worship, to read God's Word, or even to pray. Others in the body of Christ, not understanding the battle that rages in the mind of those in bondage, often say, "You just need to read your Bible more, pray harder." But when you are in bondage, you surrender your freedom and lose your right to choose.

You become like Paul in Romans 7:19: "For what I do is not the good I want to do; no, the evil I do not want to do—this I keep on doing." Finding your freedom in Christ gives you back your right to choose. Now you can read and understand God's Word, because you have submitted to Him and closed the door to the enemy.

Just because you secured your freedom in Christ doesn't mean the enemy will now roll over and play dead. He doesn't give up. He can still tempt you, accuse you, and even deceive you if you let him. He is like the scary image of the wizard of Oz. The self-proclaiming, powerful, and wonderful Oz, while in reality nothing more than smoke and mirrors, could get people to believe a lie—that he was more powerful than he really was. When the little dog Toto pulled back the curtain and exposed Oz, the lie and the power of Oz was broken; he was just a little man from Kansas and a deceiver.

When you find your freedom in Christ, you don't have to say yes to sin any longer. You are free to take God's way of escape. You can now see through Satan's smoke and mirrors, uncover his lies, and destroy his power and influence over you. But he will continue to try to deceive you.

You can't expect Mom, Dad, your pastor, or your youth pastor to fight the battle for you. They don't always know when you're being tempted, accused, or deceived. It's your mind and your battle. Only Christ can be your true strength, only He knows what you're thinking and feeling. Jesus is the one who can reveal to your mind what you need to confess and renounce, and only Jesus can help you maintain your freedom at the deepest level.

If you are being set free from deep-seated bondages that have gone undisturbed for years, you may be battle weary. Hold on, don't get lazy and slip back into them.

You now have your freedom of choice back. It's important that, during this time of newfound freedom, you take careful steps to renew your mind. That's what this book is all about. When you found your freedom in Christ, you also discovered your authority in Christ to tell the enemy to get, and to take every thought captive to the obedience of Christ. So now it is time to put your freedom to work, to get into God's Word, memorize scripture, pray, fast, and worship God. All the things you couldn't do before are now yours to participate in freely.

You have secured your freedom by asking God to reveal what has kept you in bondage. You have confessed, forgiven, and renounced the lies you believed. Still, the enemy will regroup and make a second charge at you.

Many who have gone through the *Steps to Freedom* have shared with us that days later the enemy tried to reclaim lost territory. One person told us, "I just don't feel free. I know there must be something else I need to confess and renounce. I've asked God to show me what it is, but nothing comes to my mind."

God is merciful and may not reveal everything at once, or He may wait until we are ready to deal with it. But He never leaves us with a lack of peace or the sense that something is missing. If God isn't revealing anything to your mind for repentance, then there is nothing to confess and renounce. You're free. You may not feel free, but remember, we don't walk according to our feeling. We are called to walk according to the truth regardless of how we feel. We have very little control over how we feel, but we can always choose to believe the truth. We must stay sharp and use the authority that we have in Christ to tell the enemy to get if we even suspect he is trying to influence us.

Say the following statements out loud:

THE LIE TO REJECT:

I reject the lie that I am unable to resist the devil.

THE TRUTH TO ACCEPT:

I accept the truth that in Christ I am able to stand firm in my faith.

PRAYER FOR TODAY:

Dear heavenly Father, Thank You for overcoming the enemy. I know that You defeated Satan through Your work on the cross. Because I have accepted You as my Savior, I now recognize that he has no power over me unless I disobey Your word and open doors to the enemy's influence. Please reveal to my mind if I have opened any doors to the enemy in my life. I want to believe Your truth and reject the enemy's lies. In Jesus' name I pray. Amen.

DAY TWENTY-TWO

For God has not given us a spirit of fear, but of power and of love and of a sound mind (2 Timothy 1:7 NKJV).

Fear always has an object. We may fear heights, fire, small spaces, air travel or things that threaten us. In order for a fear object to be legitimate, it must have two qualities: It must be powerful as well as present.

I (Dave) remember being in Africa and hearing the Swahili word for snake. When you hear the word "snake" you pay attention because they have some very interesting snakes over there. One day a little girl said she had seen a snake and asked if we could come and kill it. I'm not for just killing snakes, but this one happened to be a green mamba. The Africans call it the three-step snake; if it bites, you have about three steps before you're dead. The next moment, as I stared up at the seven-foot green mamba in the tree, you might imagine that I had a healthy fear of that snake. Why? Because it was present and powerful. As I sit here recalling the event, however, I don't sense any fear at all. The reason, of course, is that there are no snakes present. But if you were to open my study door and throw one toward my feet, my fear index would rise from 0 to 10 immediately. That snake would be both present and powerful! After we killed the snake and removed its head, we all posed for the camera, bravely holding the reptile with our bare hands, un-afraid. Why weren't we afraid? Because the snake had lost one of the attributes of fear. It was present but not powerful. It was dead, headless, unable to bite and use its lethal poison. To resolve the fear in your life, you must remove either the fear object's presence or its power.

Fear is a powerful controller, compelling us to do what is irresponsible or destructive. You may have heard the following story about a woman named Sarah. Her story shows how fear can control us if we don't recognize the power and presence of Christ.

Sarah was more than rich, she was a millionaire. She was very popular and powerful, but she lived in fear.

Her only daughter had died at just five weeks of age. Then, to make matters even worse, her husband passed away, as well.

With nothing to tie her down and no reason to stay at her home in New Haven, Connecticut, Sarah decided to move out West. It was 1884, and the West had been won, thanks to the cavalry and their advanced weapons. So she wasn't afraid of the West; it was another kind of fear that drove her to San Jose, California.

Her fear controlled her, imprisoned her, bound her; she yearned for freedom.

She saw an eight-room farmhouse and 160 acres of land and bought it. What she did then was driven by her deep and secret fears. She hired dozens of carpenters and put them to work on a mansion that would destroy fear.

Sarah's floor plan was just plain spooky. Each window was to have 13 panes, each wall 13 panels, each closet 13 hooks, and each chandelier 13 globes. Thirteen was incorporated whenever possible.

Corridors snaked randomly, some leading nowhere. One door opened to a blank wall, another to a 50-foot drop. One set of stairs led to a ceiling that had no door. Trap doors. Secret passageways. Tunnels. This was no retirement home for Sarah's future; it was a castle for dealing with her secret fears.

The making of this mansion of fear only ended when Sarah died.

Why did Sarah build such a mansion? Didn't she live alone? "Well sort of," those acquainted with her story might answer. "There were visitors. . . ."

And the visitors came each night.

One of the many legends says that every evening at midnight, the spirits would come and haunt Sarah. Unable to sleep, she would travel the twisted corridors of the house, hoping the spirits would be confused by the labyrinth of passageways and be unable to haunt her. They would linger until 2:00 A.M., when a bell would be rung by one of the servants. Then Sarah could rest. Sarah would return to her quarters, and according to legend, the ghosts would return to their graves.

Who made up this legion of phantoms? Was it the Indians and soldiers killed on the U.S. frontier, who had been killed by bullets from the most popular rifle in America—the Winchester? What had brought millions of dollars to Sarah Winchester had brought death to them.

So Sarah spent her remaining years in a mansion of fear, trying to trick the dead.

Do I believe Sarah saw ghosts? No. If she saw anything at all, they were deceiving spirits who were happy to play on her fears and appear as Indians and soldiers. If she had known Christ and her authority in Him, she could have stopped the endless building and sent the spirits away with a single verbal prayer.

In our experience, when young people have an overwhelming sense of fear and dread with no discernible reason, the cause is the enemy.

People often ask us why we aren't afraid of Satan in our line of ministry. We tell them, "There is not a verse in the Bible where we are told to fear Satan." His strategy is to roar like a hungry lion, seeking someone to devour. He roars so that he might paralyze his prey in fear.

The fear of Satan is far more present than we ever care to realize. But it has been our privilege to see hundreds of young people freed from this fear.

Not only are we not to fear Satan, but we are not to fear other people or even death. Matthew 10:28 tells us, "Do not be afraid of those who kill the body but cannot kill the soul. Rather, be afraid of the one who can destroy both soul and body in hell." People are not legitimate fear objects for a Christian. Too many times we let them intimidate us to the point of losing self-control. When this happens, the spirit of God no longer controls us, nor do we exercise self-control. We allow an unhealthy fear, instead of faith, to control our lives.

Even death is not a legitimate fear object. Hebrews 9:27 says, ". . . man is destined to die once, and after that to face judgment." Death is imminent, but God has removed its power over us. As 1 Corinthians 15:54,55 says, "Death has been swallowed up in victory. Where, O death, is your victory? Where, O death, is your sting?" The person who is freed from the fear of death is free to live today.

There is, however, one legitimate and ultimate fear in our lives—the fear of God. That's because He is *both* omnipresent and omnipotent. And the fear of God can expel all other fears. "Do not call conspiracy everything that these people call conspiracy; do not fear what they fear, and do not dread it. The Lord Almighty is the one you are to regard as holy, he is the one you are to fear, he is the one you are to dread, and he will be a sanctuary" (Isaiah 8:12-14).

To fear God is to ascribe to Him those attributes that become the basis for sanctuary, a place of safety in this lifetime. We need to understand, however, that the fear of God does not involve punishment. We don't fear God because some day He will punish us—God the Father already allowed Christ to take our punishment for our sins. "There is no fear in love. But perfect love drives out fear, because fear has to do with punishment. The one who fears is not made perfect in love" (1 John 4:18). We need to reverentially fear God as the Lord of the universe and the Lord of our lives, and humbly bow before Him. When we, with reverence and awe, make God our ultimate fear object and set up Christ as the Lord of our lives, we will experience the freedom that Christ purchased for us on the cross.

The Lie to Reject:

I reject the lie that I must live in fear of man, death, or Satan.

The Truth to Accept:

I accept the truth that no one is more present and powerful than God, so I never need to fear man, death, or Satan.

Prayer for Today:

Dear heavenly Father, I acknowledge You as the only legitimate fear object in my life. You are all powerful and present everywhere. Because of Your love and the finished work of Christ, I no longer fear punishment. I sanctify You as the Lord of my life and claim the spirit of power, love, and a sound mind that comes from Your presence in my life. I renounce Satan as a fear object in my life, and I renounce all his lies that would hold me in fear. Show me how I have allowed the fear of people and the fear of death to control my life. I now commit myself to You, and worship only You as my loving heavenly Father, that I may be guided by faith and not by fear. I ask this in the precious name of Jesus. Amen.

DAY TWENTY-THREE

We know that anyone born of God does not continue to sin; the one who was born of God keeps him safe, and the evil one cannot harm him. We know that we are children of God, and that the whole world is under the control of the evil one. We know also that the Son of God has come and has given us understanding, so that we may know him who is true. And we are in him who is true—even in his Son Jesus Christ. He is the true God and eternal life (1 John 5:18-20).

Several years ago, a Christian counselor asked if I (Neil) would sit in on one of his cases. He had been counseling a young woman for about four years, with little progress. He wondered if the girl's problem might be a demonic one; he admitted that he had no experience in dealing with that. She had pentagrams cut into her skin, and many other physical evidences of satanic ritual abuse. I thought, *That's a clue!*

After being with her for just a few minutes, I said, "There is a battle going on for your mind."

"Oh praise God," she said, "finally somebody understands."

The next week she came into my office, and as we talked, this large lady suddenly became disoriented, got out of her chair, and walked toward me. What would you do in that situation? I looked at her and said to the deceptive forces that had overcome her, "I am a child of God, you can't touch me" (see 1 John 5:18). She stopped in her tracks. I told her to sit down, and she returned to her chair.

By the way, authority does not increase with volume. We don't have to shout down the devil; we can quietly take our authority in Christ.

I shared this story with a group on the East Coast, and several weeks later a doctoral student approached me and thanked me for that illustration. He said, "Just the other morning I was down at the commuter station waiting for my ride, when three thugs came up and demanded my money. Neil, it was like I could look right through them. So I said very confidently, 'I am a child of God, and the evil one cannot touch me.' The three thieves said, 'What?' I said again, 'I am a child of God, and the evil one cannot touch me.' They said, 'Oh,' and walked away." This student discerned the true source of his opposition, which was spiritual.

People with spiritual problems usually have a common problem—they lack a true understanding of their identity in Christ. If the whole world is under the control of the evil one, then the *only* legitimate safety we have is *in Christ*. In the passage that began today's time, John repeatedly says, "We know . . . we know . . . we know." In each case, he refers to the assurance that is ours as children of God.

We cannot use ritualistic slogans or trite formulas to win our battle with the evil one, as some spiritual impostors found out in Acts 19:13-16:

> Some Jews who went around driving out evil spirits tried to invoke the name of the Lord Jesus over those who were demon-possessed. They would say, "In the name of Jesus, whom Paul preaches, I command you to come out." Seven sons of Sceva, a Jewish chief priest, were doing this. One day the evil spirit answered them, "Jesus I know, and I know about Paul, but who are you?" Then the man who had the evil spirit jumped on them and overpowered them all. He gave them such a beating that they ran out of the house naked and bleeding.

Have you ever awakened at night feeling terrorized? You may have felt a pressure on your chest or an evil presence in the room. Perhaps you tried to respond but couldn't. At virtually every conference we have led around the world, between one-third to one-half of the young people have experienced such an attack. It is, of course, no sin to be under attack, just as it is no sin to be tempted. But what should you do? First, remember what 2 Corinthians 10:4 says: "The weapons we fight with are not the weapons of the world."

Initially, you may feel powerless to respond physically. I believe God may be allowing this for our testing.

It is as though He is saying, "Go ahead, try to get out of this by yourself, see what you can do." But we can't. We absolutely need God. The Bible says that those who call upon the name of the Lord shall be saved. But how can you call upon the name of the Lord if you're speechless? The answer is in James 4:7: "Submit yourselves, then, to God. Resist the devil, and he will flee from you."

God knows the thoughts and intentions of your heart. Regardless of what is happening around you, you can always direct your inward thoughts toward Him. As soon as you acknowledge His authority in your life, you will be released to call upon the Lord. All you have to say is, "Jesus." But you have to *say it out loud*. Satan is under no obligation to obey your thoughts; he doesn't perfectly know them. Only God is omniscient. Never ascribe the divine attributes of God to Satan. He is a created being, not the Creator.

The devil is the father of lies, and his power is in the lie. But the truth sets us free. When you expose the lie, you break the power of it. For the Christian, power lies in the truth. Nowhere does the Bible tell us we are to pursue power in this world. Why? Because we already possess it. The apostle Paul prayed that our eyes would be opened and we come to know the power we already have (see Ephesians 1:18,19).

Because of our position in Christ, we have the authority and the responsibility to resist the devil. But trying to do so without first submitting to God will end in a power struggle. On the other hand, submitting to God without resisting the devil may leave you in bondage. Remember, James 4:7 tells us to first submit to God, and then assume our responsibility to resist the devil.

Habitual and unrepentant sin accumulates like garbage, and garbage attracts rats. The tendency is to drive off the rats, but they will only come back. The key is to get rid of the garbage; then the rats have no reason to return.

The one born of God does not continue in sin. He will be under the conviction of the Holy Spirit, who will always drive him back to God. Even if you are struggling in your Christian walk, you can know that you are safe in the arms of God. The evil one cannot touch those who are in Christ. We ought to have enough confidence in God and His Word to say, "I know I am a child of God, that I have been bought and purchased by the blood of Jesus Christ, that I am in Christ, and that nothing can separate me from the love of God."

We encourage you to read *Stomping Out the Darkness* and *The Bondage Breaker Youth Edition* for more on this subject.

Our only safety is found in Christ. As 1 John 5:13 says, "I write these things to you who believe in the name of the Son of God so that you may know that you have eternal life." This is the confidence God wants us to have, this is our sanctuary.

The Lie to Reject:

I reject the lie that I am powerless and under Satan's control.

The Truth to Accept:

I accept the truth that I am in Christ and not subject to the god of this world.

Prayer for Today:

Dear heavenly Father, I thank You for my security in Christ. The evil one cannot touch me. I bring all the garbage that I have gathered in my life before You; I no longer desire to live in sin. I now choose to receive Your conviction and seek Your cleansing as I confess my sins. I will assume my responsibility to put on the armor of God and resist the devil. I renounce the lies of Satan that I am powerless and under his control. I am in Christ and not subject to the god of this world. By Your grace I am Your child, and You will keep me safe. In Jesus' precious name I pray. Amen.

——— Day Twenty-Four ———

But the fruit of the Spirit is love, joy, peace, patience, kindness, goodness, faithfulness, gentleness and self-control. Against such things there is no law. Those who belong to Christ Jesus have crucified the sinful nature with its passions and desires. Since we live by the Spirit, let us keep in step with the Spirit (Galatians 5:22-25).

One of Satan's favorite lies is, "Try harder!" But living out your freedom in Christ is not just a matter of self-determination. Trying harder didn't set you free from sin's bondage, and trying harder won't keep you free. In fact, going through a workbook doesn't set you free. Jesus Christ is the one who can set you free. As you submit to God's truth, confess, forgive, renounce the enemy's lies, and announce God's truth, you close the road of bondage and open the pathway to freedom. Galatians 5:22-25 reminds us: "But the fruit of the Spirit is love, joy, peace, patience, kindness, goodness, faithfulness, gentleness and self-control. Against such things there is no law. Those who belong to Christ Jesus have crucified the sinful nature with its passions and desires. Since we live by the Spirit, let us keep in step with the Spirit."

We maintain our freedom by choosing to believe the truth and by keeping in step with the Spirit. We can never manipulate our flesh to manifest a fruit of the Spirit. No amount of human willpower can squeeze a single drop of freedom or obedience to God out of our being. No amount of positive thinking, accountability groups, church visits, Bible reading, or prayer times can substitute for the presence of the Holy Spirit; only a personal relationship with Christ can ensure the Spirit's presence. Zechariah 4:6 says, "'Not by might nor by power, but by my Spirit,' says the LORD Almighty."

Our world tells us, "You can do it. You don't need God or anyone else. You can straighten out your own life, take care of your own problems." Oh no we can't; we absolutely need God, and we desperately need each other. We've been conditioned by the world's lies. But the world's way is not God's way. The world is subject to the god of this world—Satan. He created the lie that we are able to do things independent of God. Satan's original sin was his desire to be independent of God, to do things his own way, under his own power. But God's desire and design for us is to be totally dependent on Him. Satan's attempt to control and empower his own life led to his fall from heaven. And when Adam and Eve tried to live independent of God, they destroyed their relationship with their creator and were cast out of the garden of Eden (see Genesis 3).

When you were in bondage, you were tricked into depending on yourself or Satan's lies. But now that you're free, you're able to renew your mind and destroy every evil thought that led you to live your life independently of God (see 2 Corinthians 10:5). We can't underestimate the power of Satan's lies and the influence of the world on our minds. The world's programming and conditioning has no doubt produced independence in us that we can't even see. We have blind spots, but God is faithful to reveal to us where we are being deceived. This shows how much we desperately need Him; we can't even see our needs—let alone meet them.

Through His Word, God is able to reveal our blind spots, while at the same time rebuilding our broken relationship with Him. We often see dependence as something shameful. God, however, sees proper dependence on Him as essential for a loving, personal relationship with Him. Intimacy and closeness with God are only possible as we submit to His loving ways and declare a life of dependence on Him. When Paul asked God about a certain weakness, the Lord told him, "My grace is sufficient for you, for my power is made perfect in weakness." Paul goes on to say, "Therefore I will boast all the more gladly about my weaknesses, so that Christ's power may rest on me. That is why, for Christ's sake, I delight in weaknesses, in insults, in hardships, in persecutions, in difficulties. For when I am weak, then I am strong" (2 Corinthians 12:9,10).

We are headed for bondage when we declare our own strength and independence from God. Our self-willed independence leads to a false sense of security; we learn to trust in ourselves and not God.

Jesus doesn't want us to go through this world alone. He wants to help us through it. He is yoked to us (Matthew 11:29,30). But to put on Jesus' yoke you first need to cast off every other yoke and declare your need for Jesus' yoke or strength. You and Jesus are now tied together. You would never yoke two different kinds of animals together, like an ox and a mule. One would break its neck because they move at different paces. Jesus' illustration implies that you are created in the image of God. Now you're a child of God who is alive in the Spirit. Now you can keep in step with the Spirit.

When we combine our strength with God's strength and the strength of the body of Christ, we become a cord of three strands. "Though one may be overpowered, two can defend themselves. A cord of three strands is not quickly broken" (Ecclesiastes 4:12).

THE LIE TO REJECT:

I reject the lie that I am able to live the Christian life in my own strength and power.

THE TRUTH TO ACCEPT:

I accept the truth that only in Christ am I able to walk free and please God.

PRAYER FOR TODAY:

Dear heavenly Father, I confess that at times I have tried to live the Christian life under my own power. But I know that only through Your Holy Spirit's power am I able to walk free and please You. Lord, I confess and renounce my self-determination and agree that not by my might nor by my power can I walk free, but only by Your Spirit. Lord, I here and now declare my total and complete dependence on You. I proclaim that apart from Christ I can do nothing. Only through Your truth am I set free from my sins and bondage. Thank You for the power to live by Your Holy Spirit and the guidance into all truth. I believe that I am spiritually strong, not because of my strength, but because Jesus is my strength. Thank You that I am yoked to Jesus and that Your yoke is my strength. Thank You that Your yoke is easy. Lord, I ask You to bring a fresh movement of Your Spirit upon me that I may keep in step with the Spirit. In Jesus' name I pray. Amen.

DAY TWENTY-FIVE

Now it is God who makes both us and you stand firm in Christ. He anointed us, set his seal of ownership on us, and put his Spirit in our hearts as a deposit, guaranteeing what is to come (2 Corinthians 1:21,22).

We are living in a nation where authority is questioned and leaders are challenged—there is a lack of trust, a spirit of unbelief.

But does losing our faith in humanity mean our ability to trust God is altered? "What if some did not have faith? Will their lack of faith nullify God's faithfulness?

Not at all! Let God be true, and every man a liar" (Romans 3:3,4).

Numbers 23:19 says, "God is not a man, that he should lie," and Hebrews 6:18 tells us, "It is impossible for God to lie."

Manmade kingdoms come and go, human authorities rise and fall. However, the integrity of the church is not based on the fickle nature of man or the credibility of human government; nor is our relationship with God based on that. Rather, the integrity of the church and our relationship with God are based upon His faithfulness and the assurance of His Word.

"Now it is God who makes both us and you stand firm in Christ" (2 Corinthians 1:21). God is the one who establishes us. How does He do this? First, He anoints us. *Cristos*, the Greek word for Christ, means "the anointed one." In our opening passage, the word anointed is the Greek word *Chrio*, which is used in the Septuagint (a Greek translation of the Old Testament before the time of Christ) for kings, priests, and prophets. This is kingdom terminology; someone is anointed for some regal position. Peter captures this idea when he declares, "But you are a chosen people, a royal priesthood, a holy nation, a people belonging to God, that you may declare the praises of him who called you out of darkness into his wonderful light" (1 Peter 2:9). We are not speaking here of a temporal kingdom; this is God's *eternal* Kingdom, and God *Himself* has anointed us to be a part of it.

Not only that, God has set His seal of ownership upon us. Historically, kings and other royalty used seals as a means of communicating the integrity and authority of a message. They would pour melted wax upon a letter that was folded closed. Then they would seal it with an impression of their ring or another official insignia stamped into the wax. Once the letter was opened and the seal was broken, you could no longer ensure its contents.

We have in our country a seal that signifies the rights and privileges of citizenship, but Christians have a greater seal given by God that ensures much more.

We have been bought and purchased by the blood of the Lamb. God has placed His seal upon us, ensuring His protection through any enduring trials or judgment, both now and forever.

We are God's covenant people and participants of a new covenant, not one written on stone tablets but on our hearts. "This is the covenant I will make with them after that time, says the Lord. I will put my laws in their hearts, and I will write them on their minds. . . . Their sins and lawless acts I will remember no more" (Hebrews 10:16,17).

Not only are we sealed, but God has put His Spirit in our hearts as a deposit, guaranteeing what is to come. Paul says in Ephesians 1:13,14, "And you also were included in Christ when you heard the word of truth, the gospel of your salvation. Having believed, you were marked in him with a seal, the promised Holy Spirit, who is a deposit guaranteeing our inheritance until the redemption of those who are God's possession—to the praise of his glory." This guarantee is not offered to you by some inflated politician or star-struck entertainer or even your youth pastor. *God* guarantees and ensures it by placing His Holy Spirit within us as a down payment.

Then we have the added assurance of Hebrews 13:5: "Never will I leave you; never will I forsake you." So while the questionable promises and destructive tongues of man would tear down the very fabric of society, we do well to pay heed to Ephesians 4:29,30: "Do not let any unwholesome talk come out of your mouths, but only what is helpful for building others up according to their needs, that it may benefit those who listen. And do not grieve the Holy Spirit of God, with whom you were sealed for the day of redemption."

THE LIE TO REJECT:

I reject the lie that God would or could ever lie to me.

THE TRUTH TO ACCEPT:

I accept the truth that You are a God who cannot lie and will not lie to me.

PRAYER FOR TODAY:

Dear heavenly Father, I praise You for being a God who cannot lie. Forgive me for believing the promise of man, when I should have been resting in Your promises. Forgive me for questioning Your faithfulness because of the unfaithfulness of people. I renounce the lies of Satan that question Your Word, and I submit to the Holy Spirit, who guarantees my inheritance to come. Thank You for establishing me, anointing me, placing Your seal of ownership on me, and putting Your Spirit in my heart. In Jesus' name and by the authority of His Word I pray. Amen.

Extreme Extras

Explore the Word

Write out what these verses say about you.

(Romans 5:1): _____

(Romans 6:1-6): _____

(Romans 8:1): _____

(1 Corinthians 1:30): _____

(1 Corinthians 2:12): _____

(1 Corinthians 2:16): _____

Expand Your Mind

Memorize Romans 5:1:

Therefore, since we have been justified through faith, we have peace with God through our Lord Jesus Christ.

EXPRESS YOURSELF

_____

_____

_____

_____

_____

_____

_____

_____

_____

_____

_____

_____

_____

_____

_____

_____

_____

_____

_____

_____

_____

_____

_____

_____

6

A Life of eXcellence!
Believing the Truth

DAY TWENTY-SIX

For in Him dwells all the fullness of the God-head bodily; and you are complete in Him, who is the head of all principality and power (Colossians 2:9,10 NKJV).

Suppose a brand-new car rolled off the assembly line in Detroit, advertised as the most luxurious and powerful automobile ever made. It had a spark of life in it because of the battery, but it had yet to be filled with gas. A tribesman from a remote part of the Amazon was flown in to inspect this beautiful car. Having no previous knowledge of cars, he wondered about the purpose of this object.

The tribesman observed the object's beautiful lines—the symmetry, the chrome, the paint job—and thought its value might simply be in its beauty, like a statue's. As he sat in the bucket seats, tilting them forward and moving them up and down, he wondered if the object might be for the purpose of comfort; could it be a small dwelling? He turned on the quadraphonic stereo system and thought the car was possibly created for the enjoyment of music. When he turned on the headlights and dome lights, he thought the car could be for light. Tooting the horn, he thought the car's purpose was to give a warning. Then someone filled the car with gasoline, put it in gear, and the vehicle began to move forward. Finally, the tribesman understood the real purpose for which the car was created.

The purpose of an automobile is to provide transportation, but it can only do this when it is filled with fuel. The body and accessories may be luxurious, but they won't move on their own. Nor does the engine itself have power on its own; its purpose is to convert the fuel into a usable energy force. Then, and only then, can the automobile fulfill its purpose.

We were never designed by God to function independently of Him. God created Adam and Eve spiritually alive; their souls were in union with Him. Only in this way could they fulfill the purpose for which they were created. But man has rebelled and chosen to live his life independent of God. Because of sin, he is separated from God. Without God we are incomplete. However, His plan is to present us again complete in Christ.

The young woman's testimony that follows illustrates this:

The word "handicapped" describes my family. My mother had muscular dystrophy, my father polio, and my brother cerebral palsy. Though I have had no physical problem myself, I've seen the stares and glances of people, and I've always felt like somehow our family was weird.

My father was abusive, beating us regularly. One time, in a fit of anger, he grabbed my mother's head as she sat in her wheelchair, and pounded it against the kitchen counter. He was enslaved to pornography and often called me horrible names, such as "slut" and "whore." I made a dress in sewing class once, and he tore it off me, saying only a whore would wear a dress like that.

Often I heard my mother weeping and crying out to the Lord for strength. I was slowly losing hope. By the seventh grade I was escaping through alcohol, and then through sex, which resulted in an abortion. When I was 17, my mom died, and at 18, I was out of the house and supporting myself.

I thought I could finally find some peace, but instead I felt empty and full of guilt. I didn't know what to do with my life, but I knew I needed help. I stumbled into a church one day and heard about God's forgiveness and love. I sobbed as I asked Jesus into my life. A huge weight lifted from my heavy heart, and I experienced indescribable joy. I was on a spiritual high for months as I went to Bible studies and met other Christians. But my non-Christian boyfriend kept saying I was getting weird. I didn't know much Scripture, yet, to counteract this, and I was intimidated by him. Besides, we were living together, and I felt I needed him, though I was really supporting him. When we finally got married, everything became worse. He gambled, and I resumed drinking. I hoped our first child would somehow bring the fulfillment I craved, but that didn't happen. By the time our second baby was six months old, my husband had gambled away all of our money, and I left him.

I went through months of depression and darkness. Then one night I decided to start living again; I began partying and seeking attention from men. I didn't care whether they were married or not; I just wanted someone to tell me I was okay. But after another devastating relationship, I heard the Lord say, "You don't need men to make you happy; you only need Me." But I refused to listen to God's gentle call back to Himself.

Finally, I met a wonderful man and married him. Life would surely be great now. But the first years of our marriage brought out all that was ugly in both of us. Eventually, I realized my drinking was hindering my husband who was an alcoholic, and I turned to the Lord for strength to quit. In spite of all my wrong choices and rebellion, I sensed that His love had preserved me. I felt He was telling me that if I would just start concentrating on Him, abiding in Him as my all-sufficient-one, He would take responsibility for my husband.

I found a little church with a wonderful pastor, and my husband was even willing to attend with me sometimes. The pastor's wife became my friend and discipler. One day, I realized that my husband had changed; he was kinder and more at peace. When I asked him about it, he told me he'd received Christ a few weeks before at our church. Some time later I heard him praying one night for God to deliver him from alcoholism. The Lord graciously did just that.

About that time, I attended a Freedom in Christ conference and prayed through the *Steps to Freedom* with a friend. What an eye-opening, heart-revealing, truth encounter! Forgiving my father from my heart helped me see what my true heavenly Father is like. I am no longer bound by my past. My identity is now in Christ, and I am made complete in Him. I was chosen in Christ before the foundation of the world to be holy and without blame. Daily I put on the armor of God, and I praise Him that by His grace I am what I am.

Perhaps, like this dear lady, you have gone from experience to experience seeking fulfillment and completeness.

I hope you see by now that no person or material thing can fill the vacuum inside. You were created to relate to God in soul-union, and you can only find rest and purpose in your life when you put your total dependence upon Him.

Paul says in Ephesians 5:18,19, "Do not get drunk on wine, which leads to debauchery. Instead, be filled with the Spirit. Speak to one another with psalms, hymns and spiritual songs. Sing and make music in your heart to the Lord." If we will only let ourselves be filled with the Spirit of God, we can move joyfully down the road of life, fulfilling our purpose. Wherever I am in my process of maturity, I can only accomplish things in my life if I am operating by the power of the Holy Spirit. I am complete only in Christ.

When you first became a Christian, you were like a small lawn mower engine. You could accomplish a necessary task and fulfill a worthwhile purpose. However, your goal is to mature into a giant tractor, and accomplish even greater things. And so, as you mature, remember that the small engine and the giant tractor can only do what they were made to do when the fuel is added to them. We can only fulfill our purpose for being here when we are filled with the Holy Spirit.

Our entire goal of discipleship is to work toward presenting everybody "perfect" (complete or established) in Christ (see Colossians 1:28). According to Colossians 2:10, we are already complete in Christ; *we are incomplete without Him.*

God's gracious provision and offer to all Christians is that they might have the full assurance that they are, *right now*, complete in Christ. Paul says in Colossians 1:27-29, "To them God has chosen to make known among the Gentiles the glorious riches of this mystery, which is Christ in you, the hope of glory. We proclaim him, admonishing and teaching everyone with all wisdom, so that we may present everyone perfect in Christ. To this end I labor, struggling with all his energy, which so powerfully works in me. "

THE LIE TO REJECT:

I reject the lie that I can be complete by seeking my own purposes in life.

THE TRUTH TO ACCEPT:

I accept the truth that I am now complete in Christ.

PRAYER FOR TODAY:

Dear heavenly Father, Thank You for Your love, and for making me aware that I was incomplete without You. I thank You that I am now complete in Christ. I choose to no longer seek my purpose in life in any way independent of You. I put no confidence in my own ability. I declare my dependence upon You, and seek to fulfill my purpose by asking You to fill me with Your Holy Spirit. I renounce every occasion when I have sought power or fulfillment from any source other than You. I choose to be strong in You, Lord, and in the strength of Your might. In Jesus' precious name I pray. Amen.

DAY TWENTY-SEVEN

Finally, be strong in the Lord and in his mighty power. Put on the full armor of God so that you can take your stand against the devil's schemes. For our struggle is not against flesh and blood, but against the rulers, against the authorities, against the powers of this dark world and against the spiritual forces of evil in the heavenly realms (Ephesians 6:10-12).

Spiritual forces of evil. That sounds pretty terrible, doesn't it? Often we lose touch with just how awful and destructive the enemy's work is. Let me share with you some statistics that I believe show just how powerful and evil the forces of darkness are.

EVERY 24 HOURS . . .

2,989 children watch their parents split
  apart in divorce
2,556 children are born outside of marriage
1,629 children are put into adult jails
3,288 children run away from home
1,849 children are abused or neglected
1,512 teenagers drop out of school
  437 children are arrested for drunk driving
  211 children are arrested for drug abuse
2,795 teens get pregnant
7,742 teens become sexually active
1,106 teenagers give birth
  372 teenagers miscarry
  623 teenagers contract syphilis or gonorrhea
    6 teenagers commit suicide[1]

The enemy is real and active; he has come to steal, kill, and destroy. But Jesus came to bring life, an abundant life. Sometimes we read statistics like the above and say, "What's the use of even trying to live the Christian life; it's impossible in a world like this!" Without Christ and His armor it would be impossible, but with Christ all things are possible (see Ephesians 6:11-18). Now, where do you start? You start with your belief system! A healthy Christian walk is the result of a healthy Christian belief system—not the other way around. For example, the Bible tells us to stand firm "against the devil's schemes" (Ephesians 6:11). But how can we hope to stand firm if we don't understand that God has already raised us up with Christ and seated us victoriously with Him in heavenly realms (Ephesians 2:4-6). If what we believe about God and our position is shaky, then our day-to-day behavior will be shaky. But when our belief system and our relationship with God is based on what He says is true, we'll have little trouble working out the practical aspects of daily Christianity. We *can* change the statistics we cited, but we must start by believing the truth.

At one time in history, humans believed the earth was flat. With this belief system in place, how do you think the early sailors felt about crossing the ocean? Because they believed the earth was flat, they concluded that if they sailed too far out they would fall off the face of the earth. Their fears had nothing to do with reality, but until someone actually sailed across the ocean and proved the world was round, everyone naturally stuck to the old belief system.

We know that we can stand firm against the devil's schemes because Jesus has 1) already defeated the devil at the cross; and 2) gained final victory in His resurrection and ascension. Now that's fact, but what if you mistakenly believed Satan was still strong enough to defeat you? How would you live?Probably like those early seamen, afraid and anxious.

Examine your belief system. Does it line up with the Word of God, or like those sailors of the past, do you need to go exploring? Remember, as long as you believe that God is your loving Father and you are His accepted child, your faith will give you the peaceful assurance of God's unconditional love and acceptance. If you don't accept that truth, you'll struggle to earn acceptance that is already yours in Christ.

Whenever I (Dave) go to the beach, I inevitably see someone with a metal detector combing the sand, trying to find lost jewelry or coins. Soon I hear that loud beeping, squawking sound that makes everybody on the beach turn around to see what the person has found. Wouldn't it be great if God gave us a truth detector, an alarm that would sound inside our heads, saying, "That's a lie!" or "You got it , that's the truth." Well, you have all the equipment you need to change your belief system and bring it into alignment with the truth. The Bible and the Holy Spirit are able to expose any lies hidden in your belief system, and will lead you into all truth. John 14:16,17 says, "And I will ask the Father, and he will give you another Counselor to be with you forever—the Spirit of truth. The world cannot accept him, because it neither sees him nor knows him. But you know him, for he lives with you and will be in you." We do have a truth detector inside us—God the Holy Spirit, and He promises never to leave us. He will always be there to guide us into all truth.

Take some time now to ask yourself if there is any area of your life you are struggling with in your walk of faith.

What lie or deception are you believing?
What Bible truth is needed to replace that lie?

THE LIE TO REJECT:

I reject the lie that I can live the Christian life without God and His truth.

THE TRUTH TO ACCEPT:

I accept the truth that God's Word is unfailing and that what it says about me is true.

PRAYER FOR TODAY:

Dear heavenly Father, Thank You for Your Word, the Bible, and the Holy Spirit that always leads me to Your truth. I know that my belief system must reflect what your Word says or I'll really struggle to live out my faith. Thank You for always telling the truth, and giving me Your truth in a way that I can understand. I know that, when I choose to believe what You have said in Your Word, my life will be filled with peace even when times are tough. Help me to stay in Your Word. In Jesus' name. Amen.

DAY TWENTY-EIGHT

Walk by the Spirit, and you will not carry out
the desire of the flesh. For the flesh sets its desire
against the Spirit, and the Spirit against the flesh;
for these are in opposition to one another, so that
you may not do the things that you please. But if
you are led by the Spirit, you are not under the Law
(Galatians 5:16-18 NASB).

You may have read the last phrase of Galatians 5:18,
"You are not under the Law," and exclaimed,"Wow! I'm
free! Walking in the Spirit means I can do anything I
want!" Not at all. That's called "license," a total disregard
for God's loving guidelines. To be led by the Spirit means
you are free to do the right thing and to live a responsible life—something you couldn't do when you were the
prisoner of your flesh.

Søron Kierkegaard wrote a story once about a wild
duck that was flying northward and on his way, happened to land in a barnyard. He enjoyed the corn and
fresh water and so decided to stay for an hour. This place
was so awesome that he then decided to stay for a day,
then for a week, and finally for a month. At the end of
that time he thought about flying to join his friends, but
he enjoyed the safety of the barnyard and all the great
food. So he decided to hang out for the whole summer.

One autumn day, he heard his friends flying south. It
stirred him with delight, and he enthusiastically flapped
his wings and rose into the air to join them. But he found
that he could rise no higher than the barn. He muttered
to himself, "I'm satisfied here. I have plenty of food, and

the fare is good. Why should I leave?" So he stayed for the winter.

In the spring, when the wild ducks flew overhead again, he felt the stirring, but he did not even try to fly up to meet them. And when they returned in the fall, the duck did not even notice them; there was no stirring within his breast. He simply kept on eating the corn which had made him fat.[2]

Like the wild duck many young Christians surrender their freedom in Christ to enjoy the temporary pleasures of the world, only to find that they are soon in bondage to them. The pleasures of the world are real, exciting, and tempting, but they have a great price attached to them. What is your freedom worth? What would you be willing to exchange for your relationship with Christ? Hopefully nothing!

Jesus offers us the freedom of walking in the Spirit and following Him. There truly is no greater joy or peace than knowing you're keeping in step with the Spirit. Walking in the Spirit is the process of getting to know God and learning to trust Him as He helps you grow into a spiritual person. We can't drift lazily along in life and expect to live victoriously over the flesh and sin. We need to get to know God, and who we are as children of God. Think for a moment. How well do you know God—and not just facts about Him? How well do you relate to Him? How you answer that question will determine what your walk in the Spirit is like.

How do you know if you're being led by the Spirit or the flesh? What is the fruit of the Spirit? Does any particular verse or verses come to mind?

If you discover that you have followed the flesh rather than the Spirit, admit it and correct it. Take some time now to ask God to reveal any areas you need to confess and renounce. When you confess a failure and renounce it, God lovingly restores you to the place where you can grow spiritually once again and walk free.

THE LIE TO REJECT:

I reject the lie that the world, the flesh, or the devil can keep me from walking in the Spirit.

THE TRUTH TO ACCEPT:

I accept the truth that I can manifest the full fruit of the Spirit because Jesus has given me His life and the Holy Spirit lives in me.

PRAYER FOR TODAY:

Dear heavenly Father, Thank You for sending Your Son as Savior and Shepherd. Thank You for Your forgiveness when I stumble and stray. Teach me, Father, how to walk in the Spirit and to not carry out the sinful desires of the flesh. I want to be more sensitive to You. Your love and grace toward me is so awesome, I want to enjoy an even richer relationship with You so I choose to walk according to Your Spirit. In Jesus' name I pray. Amen.

DAY TWENTY-NINE

Not that we are competent to claim anything for ourselves, but our competence comes from God. He has made us competent as ministers of a new covenant—not of the letter but of the Spirit; for the letter kills, but the Spirit gives life (2 Corinthians 3:5,6).

Once I (Neil) was invited to speak to a religion class. At the end of my talk, an athletic-looking, streetwise student raised his hand and asked, "Do you have a lot of don'ts in your church?"

"What you mean is, do we have any freedom?"

He nodded.

"Sure, I'm free to do whatever I want to do. I can rob a bank. But I would be in bondage to that act for the rest of my life. I'd have to cover up my crime, go into hiding, or eventually pay for what I did. I'm also free to tell a lie. But if I do, I have to keep telling it, and I have to remember who I told it to, and how I told it, or I will get caught. I'm free to do drugs, get drunk, and live a sexually immoral lifestyle. All of those 'freedoms' lead to bondage. I'm free to make those choices, but considering the consequences, would I really be free?"

What appears to be freedom to some people isn't really freedom, but a return to bondage. Galatians 5:1 reminds us that, "It is for freedom that Christ has set us free. Stand firm, then, and do not let yourselves be burdened again by a yoke of slavery."

God's laws are not designed to tie you down and strangle you but to protect you. Your real freedom is in your ability to choose to live right within the protective guidelines God has given us.

Walking in the Spirit is not just obeying a bunch of rules. Trying to make myself spiritual by obeying every Christian rule and regulation will only result in defeat. Second Corinthians 3:6 states: "He has made us competent as ministers of a new covenant—not of the letter but of the Spirit; for the letter kills, but the Spirit gives life."

Laying down the law—telling someone it is wrong to do this or that—does not give that person the power to stop doing it. Romans 7:5 says, "When we were controlled by the sinful nature [Flesh], the sinful passions aroused by the law were at work in our bodies, so that we bore fruit for death."

You can't develop a Spirit-filled heart by doing good things. Performing Christian deeds such as studying the Bible, praying, and witnessing do not equal spiritual maturity. While these activities are good and essential for spiritual growth, they do not guarantee a Spirit-filled walk. You don't become Spirit-filled by obeying the law; you become Spirit-filled in order to obey the law.

Does this mean we can ignore the rules for behavior in the Bible? Of course not. God's law is a necessary, protective standard and guideline. Within God's law, we are free to develop a spirit-to-Spirit relationship with God.

Can you think of an example from your life or a friend's life of a time when you discovered an apparent act of freedom that instead led to bondage?

You may have been the victim of legalism, self-imposed or brought on by others. But walking in the Spirit is not legalism—that is, obeying a bunch of rules.

THE LIE TO REJECT:

I reject the lie that the law can give me the life I need. I reject legalism. I also reject the lie that God's guidelines are of no value.

THE TRUTH TO ACCEPT:

I accept the truth that Jesus Christ fulfilled the law, and that in Christ I am able to do the Father's will and obey His loving guidelines for my life and ministry by the power of the Holy Spirit.

PRAYER FOR TODAY:

Dear heavenly Father, Thank You for Your protective standards and guidelines. Within Your law I know that I'm free to develop a spirit-to-Spirit relationship with You. I know that merely doing activities does not guarantee a Spirit-filled walk. I accept the truth that Jesus fulfilled the law and that, because I'm in Christ, I have the power to obey You and follow Your will for my life. Please fill me with Your Holy Spirit so that I won't carry out the desires of the flesh.

DAY THIRTY

*Come to me, all you who are weary and burdened,
and I will give you rest. Take my yoke upon you and
learn from me, for I am gentle and humble in heart,
and you will find rest for your souls. For my yoke is
easy and my burden is light (Matthew 11:28-30).*

The Spirit-filled walk is neither license (doing what
you want) nor legalism (strict rules and regulations) but
liberty, the freedom to be who we already are in Christ:
loved, accepted children of God (see 2 Corinthians 3:6-17).

Your freedom in Christ is one of the most precious
gifts God gives you. Because of it you can choose to walk
according to the Spirit. But bondage causes you to walk
according to the flesh.

To walk according to the Spirit does not imply laziness on our part. Laziness—just putting your mind in
neutral and coasting—is one of the most dangerous and
harmful things to your spiritual growth. A lot of teens I
(Dave) have talked to have actually taken certain courses
at school that teach them how to put their minds in neutral, how to clear their minds. But that's dangerous.
When you put your mind in neutral, you open yourself
up to demonic influence. Nowhere in the Bible does it
say that God wants to bypass our minds. Nowhere in the
Bible does God ever ask us to clear our minds and put
them in neutral. Rather, the phrase "think on these
things" keeps showing up.

Many people mistakenly think that the harder they
work for God, the more spiritual they will become. That's
a lie from the enemy. The Spirit-filled life is not achieved
through endless, exhausting activity. Satan knows that he

may not be able to stop you from serving God by making you immoral, but he can probably slow you down by making you busy. A lot of teenagers I meet have so much going on that they have little time for God. God may want you to thin out your schedule so you can spend more time with Him.

Read Matthew 11:28-30 again. It contains a description of the purpose and pace of the Spirit-filled walk.

Just as two oxen walk together under the same yoke, Jesus invites you to a restful walk with Him. "How can a yoke be restful?" you ask. Because Jesus' yoke is an easy yoke. As the lead ox, Jesus walks at a steady pace. If you pace yourself with Him, your burden will be easy. If you take a passive approach to the relationship, you'll be painfully dragged along because Jesus keeps walking. If you try to race ahead or turn off in another direction, the yoke will cut into your neck and your life will be uncomfortable. The key to a restful yoke-relationship with Jesus is to learn from Him and open yourself to His gentleness and humility.

The picture of walking in the Spirit together with Jesus also helps us understand our service to God. How much can you get done without Jesus pulling on His side of the yoke? Nothing. And how much can be accomplished without you on your side? Nothing. God has chosen to work in partnership with you to do His work in the world today.

In order to put on the easy yoke that Jesus talks about, you must take off all other yokes. What other yokes do you need to shed in order to put on Christ's yoke?

Farmers always yoke together two animals of like kind. You never yoke an ox with a mule because one would break its neck because of the difference in pace.

You're yoked to Christ. That means you are like Jesus; you're of like kind.

Remember, the key to a restful relationship yoked to Jesus is to learn from Him and to open yourself to His gentleness and humility. With that kind of yoke you'll find serving God is easier than you have ever imagined.

What's your reaction to the idea that you are of like kind with Jesus and that you are yoked in partnership with Him?

The Lie to Reject:

I reject the lie that my life and ministry has to be a frenzied run from one activity to another to try to please God.

The Truth to Accept:

I accept the truth that I am yoked to Jesus; that His yoke is easy and that I can accomplish what He wants done as we walk together.

Prayer for Today:

Dear heavenly Father, Thank You for showing me what walking in the Spirit is like. Help me to stay in pace with Jesus as I am yoked to Him. Thank You for the spiritual life that You have given me, that I'm in union with You and "in Christ." I choose to shed all other yokes and put on the yoke that Christ gives me. Thank You, Lord, that Your yoke is easy and not a burden for me and that You share this yoke with me. In Jesus' name I pray. Amen.

EXTREME EXTRAS

EXPLORE THE WORD

Write out what these verses say about you.

(1 Corinthians 6:19,20): _____

(2 Corinthians 1:21; Ephesians 1:13,14): _____

(2 Corinthians 5:14,15): _____

(2 Corinthians 5:21): _____

(Galatians 2:20): _____

(Ephesians 1:3,4): _____

EXPAND YOUR MIND

Memorize Galatians 2:20:

I have been crucified with Christ and I no longer live, but Christ lives in me. The life I live in the body, I live by faith in the Son of God, who loved me and gave himself for me.

EXPRESS YOURSELF

_____

_____

_____

_____

_____

_____

_____

_____

_____

_____

_____

_____

_____

_____

_____

_____

_____

_____

_____

_____

_____

_____

_____

7

eXecutive Orders
Power in Your Ministry

As God's fellow workers we urge you not to receive God's grace in vain. For he says, 'In the time of my favor I heard you, and in the day of salvation I helped you.' I tell you, now is the time of God's favor, now is the day of salvation (2 Corinthians 6:1,2).

I (Neil) served the Lord as a seminary "prof" for 10 years, helping to equip God's coworkers. I was always frustrated by the educational system, because it afforded little time to teach the way Jesus taught—by example. He walked with His disciples during the normal course of life. The best kind of learning takes place in the context of committed relationships.

Fortunately, I did have the opportunity to get close to a few students. One of them was Stu. Stu signed up for a summer class I was teaching, but never showed up. When I saw him at the beginning of the fall semester, I asked about his absence.

"Can we talk?" he asked, straining to keep back the tears. "I was in the hospital this summer, and they diagnosed me with cancer. They say I have from six months to two years to live." He asked me not to discuss his illness with anyone, saying that even his church family didn't know.

A month later, he asked me if I believed in prophecies. "Ten years ago, a man stood up in our fellowship and said that I was going to have a significant ministry. But I haven't had a significant ministry—at least not yet. Does that mean I'm going to be healed? I have led a few hundred people to Christ, but I'm not having a significant ministry in my little church."

I was flabbergasted! "Stu," I exclaimed, "you have led a few hundred people to Christ! That's very significant! I know of some big-name people who can't come close to matching that."

The next spring, he stopped me in the hall and said he was losing weight, and he knew it wasn't fat he was losing. He thought he was dying. I told him he needed to share this with our class, that God never intended for us to walk through trials alone. He did share his news that afternoon in what turned out to be the most incredible two-hour class in my seminary experience. He expressed his pain and frustration at having to leave his wife alone. Suddenly, the issues of life and death and our work for the Lord were real to all of us.

"And all I want to do is graduate this spring," he said. "No one in my family has ever amounted to anything." We gathered around him to pray, and he added, "I totally forgot about that prophecy, but I have been telling every one of my fellow pastors, 'Do you know what Dr. Anderson said? He said there are some big-name people who can't say they have led a few hundred people to Christ.'"

The most meaningful graduation I have ever attended was that spring when Stu walked forward to receive his diploma.

I was in Philadelphia two years later when my wife called with the news that Stu had died; he had asked me to conduct his funeral. He is now with the Lord and will spend eternity along with the few hundred people he led to Christ—and the Lord only knows how many others the few hundred have touched as they continue on as coworkers with God. That's significant!

Maybe you think you're too young or don't know enough of the Bible to have an effective ministry. Maybe your sphere of influence is small. Well, age, knowledge of God's Word, and influence are important, but listen to what 2 Corinthians 6:2 says: "Now is the time of God's favor." You will receive grace to be what He has called you to be. Don't worry about the size of your ministry; size does not determine significance in the eyes of God. Your significance is found in being Christ's coworker. Every one of us has the unfathomable privilege of being a coworker with our Lord. God has extended to us the opportunity to participate with Him in His redeeming work here on earth.

Laboring with Christ, doing what He wants you to do, is what will determine your lasting influence, and, therefore, your significance. Study the Word of God, and He will give you the wisdom you need to do the ministry He's called you to. Ask God to do what He must to make you one of His most effective coworkers.

Have you ever thought your ministry was insignificant? Why or why not?

Say the following statements out loud:

THE LIE TO REJECT:

I reject the lie that I am insignificant and can have no ministry

THE TRUTH TO ACCEPT:

I accept the truth that in Christ I am significant and God's coworker.

PRAYER FOR TODAY:

Dear heavenly Father, I rejoice in being Your coworker. I gladly accept whatever assignments You give me, knowing that I will only be fulfilled by being in Your will. Forgive me for the times I have searched for significance in temporal positions and expressed dissatisfaction with my present ministry. I renounce the lies of Satan that say Your grace is not sufficient, or that You will not see me through times of hardship. When I hear the lies of Satan taunting, "Where is your God now?" I will declare that You are with me and will be with me always. I wish not to presume upon You, Lord. If what I am doing now in ministry is only my idea, done my way, I pray that You would reveal that to me. I am Your coworker—You are not mine. I want to be blessed by Your ministry, not my ministry. I now commit my ministry to You and declare You to be the head of it. I ask all this in the precious name of Jesus. Amen.

DAY THIRTY-TWO

Therefore, if anyone is in Christ, he is a new creation; the old has gone, the new has come! All this is from God, who reconciled us to himself through Christ and gave us the ministry of reconciliation: that God was reconciling the world to himself in Christ, not counting men's sins against them. And he has committed to us the message of reconciliation.

We are therefore Christ's ambassadors, as though God were making his appeal through us (2 Corinthians 5:17-20).

Because *you* are a "new creation" in Christ, *you* have a ministry of reconciliation. *You* are the bridge between a fallen humanity and a redeeming God. Nobody can reach your school, your neighborhood, and your friends like you can. We are called to be peacemakers: "Blessed are the peacemakers, for they will be called sons of God" (Matthew 5:9). You may have seen someone come into your youth group and cause problems. This person seems to have a knack for dividing the whole youth group, and in less than an hour. Any fool can divide a youth group; it takes the grace of God to unite. A simpleton can point out the character defects in another person; it takes God's perspective to see the good. A lot of young people today tear others down. "It's only a joke," they say, but how can they justify tearing others down, when the entire thrust of the New Testament is to restore a fallen humanity, to encourage the building up of one another?

If we stop walking in the Spirit, the deeds of the flesh become evident. Galatians 5:19 clearly outlines what those deeds are. But the deeds of the flesh are only the evidence. Trying to correct the symptom is trying to *fix* the flesh when we are supposed to *crucify* it (see Galatians 5:24). It's like being asked, "What improvement have you seen in your old nature since you came to Christ?" You can't improve what is in opposition to God; you can only render it inoperative (dead), and overcome it by walking according to the Spirit.

If we could see the good in people, we would be much more effective in our ministry of reconciliation. We need to catch our friends doing something good and praise them for it: "Do not let any unwholesome talk come out of your months, but only what is helpful for building others up according to their needs, that it may benefit those who listen" (Ephesians 4:29). If we memorize and put into practice this verse many of the problems in our homes and churches would dissolve overnight. Verse 30 says, "And do not grieve the Holy Spirit of God, with whom you were sealed for the day of redemption." God is grieved when we put one another down. The success of our ministry of reconciliation is directly determined by how we use our tongues—to build others up or to tear them down.

The only Christ other people see may be what they see in us. Jesus said, "All men will know that you are my disciples if you love one another" (John 13:35). I once heard the story of an anxious executive who was rushing to catch his airplane flight. As he ran through the terminal, he brushed by a little girl, knocking her and her packages to the ground. For a fleeting moment, he thought only of the plane he had to catch. Fighting the temptation to go on, he stopped and apologized. He helped the girl to her feet and made sure she was all right. She was overwhelmed by his care and concern. Looking up, she asked him, "Are you Jesus?" What an ambassador!

As we read the Gospels, we see that sinners loved to be around Jesus, and that He waged war against the hypocrites. Today, we frequently hear the criticism that the church is full of hypocrites, and that's why people stay away. This is not completely true, but true enough to cause us to examine our hearts. We cannot be both ambassadors of Christ and hypocrites, nor will we see sinners reconciled to God as long as we keep counting their sins against them. We must deal with the cause, not the symptom. Let's speak the truth in love and be known for our ministry of reconciliation.

Say the following statements out loud:

THE LIE TO REJECT:

I reject the lie of Satan that I could never be an ambassador for Christ, or have a ministry of reconciliation.

THE TRUTH TO ACCEPT:

I accept the truth that in Christ I am an ambassador for God and I am called to be an ambassador because of His presence in my life.

PRAYER FOR TODAY:

Dear heavenly Father, I thank You for sending Jesus, who took my place so I could receive salvation. Thank You for making me a new creation in Christ. I want to be a good ambassador for You. I renounce the lies of Satan that I am unqualified and unworthy to represent You. I am worthy because of Your presence in my life. Teach me to see people as You see them. Guard my mouth so that it will only be used to build up. Forgive me for the times I used my mouth to hurt instead of heal. I want to have a ministry of reconciliation, so others can be reconciled to You as I have been. I ask this in the precious name of Christ Jesus. Amen.

DAY THIRTY-THREE

Do not let any unwholesome talk come out of your mouths, but only what is helpful for building others up according to their needs, that it may benefit those who listen. And do not grieve the Holy Spirit of God, with whom you were sealed for the day of redemption (Ephesians 4:29,30).

As important as it is for you to believe in your true identity as a child of God, it's equally important that you see other Christians for who they are and treat them well. Oftentimes we think we're treating others well when, in fact, we're just deceiving ourselves.

When I (Dave) was in Africa a young man named Daniel asked me if he could buy my blue jeans. He had noticed the tear in the knee and thought that an American would probably not want them. Daniel, of course, didn't know that Americans wore them that way, and if I would just tear out the other knee I'd be in style. I told Daniel he didn't have to buy the jeans, I'd give them to him. He began to weep.

"Daniel, have I done something wrong?" I asked. "Have I offended you?"

"Oh, no!" he said. "You don't understand. It would take me a whole week to save enough money to buy these jeans. You have just saved me a whole week's pay!"

I decided then to give him some of the other extra clothes I had. I found some used T-shirts and gave them to him. Several days later I was feeling pretty good about myself. After all, I was a giving, kind person willing to give the shirt off my back, right? Wrong! I was deceived! That day I was reading in Matthew 25 and verse 40 hit me between the eyes. "The King will reply, `I tell you the truth, whatever you did for one of the least of these brothers of mine, you did for me.'"

I had given Jesus, my Savior and Lord, a pair of holey jeans and some used T-shirts and I felt good about it. I should have given Jesus my very best; I should have given Him a new pair of jeans. You and I must view other Christians as children of the most high God and treat them the way we would treat Jesus.

When we fail to see other people as children of God, it often shows up in the way we speak to them. We can easily tear others down with our words. And words hurt! One statistic states that for every positive statement you receive, you are likely to receive ten negative ones. What kind of statements are fellow Christians hearing from you? We need to see ourselves and other believers as *in Christ* and treat them as if they were Jesus Himself.

As you talk to your friends and even the people who aren't nice to you, remember, "Do not let any unwholesome talk come out of your mouths, but only what is helpful for building others up according to their needs, that it may benefit those who listen. And do not grieve the Holy Spirit of God, with whom you were sealed for the day of redemption" (Ephesians 4:29.30). Now watch what happens to your witness. As you speak kindly and lovingly to others, your ability to witness will grow and grow.

How do you feel when someone tears you down?

Why do you think it's so important that we edify (build up) and encourage one another?

Take some time to list the people in your life that you can encourage. How can you build them up?

Now list and thank God for the people who have built you up. Perhaps you should call or write and thank them for their encouragement.

THE LIE TO REJECT:

I reject the lie that I must live for myself and that I can't control what I say to others.

THE TRUTH TO ACCEPT:

I accept the truth that every Christian is in Christ, and I choose to build others up by what I say and do.

PRAYER FOR TODAY:

Dear heavenly Father, I want to follow Christ's example and build others up. Help me to watch over the words of my mouth and the things I think about. I want to encourage other believers in their walk with You. I know that, just as I'm Your special child, so is every Christian Your special child. I choose to love my brothers and sisters in Christ. Also, Lord, I ask You to increase my witness. Help me to lead people to You and not drive them away by what I say or do. In Jesus' name I pray. Amen.

DAY THIRTY-FOUR

But you will receive power when the Holy Spirit comes on you; and you will be my witnesses in Jerusalem, and in all Judea and Samaria, and to the ends of the earth (Acts 1:8).

"You will be my witnesses." What is a witness, anyway? A witness is someone who has personally seen, heard, or experienced something. The little band of apostles had seen the resurrected Jesus, but they hadn't yet experienced the power that brings new life in Christ. Just seeing the Master wasn't enough. They were told to wait until they received power from above. When the Holy Spirit came at Pentecost, they were complete. The church was born, and nothing could stand in the way—not the religious establishment of the day, not the power of the Roman government, not even the gates of hell.

Historically, the witness of the church went out first in Jerusalem, then spread to Judea, and now the gospel is heard around the world. We are fast approaching the generation that will see the fulfillment of Matthew 24:14: "And this gospel of the kingdom will be preached in the whole world as a testimony to all nations, and then the end will come."

Every child of God has the privilege of being a part of God's eternal plan. We are all personal witnesses of the power of Christ within us. So why aren't we more effective?

The first reason is ignorance. Many young people are laboring under the wrong impression that eternal life is something we get when we die. Others are ignorant of their spiritual heritage and the power we already possess. This is why Paul prays in Ephesians 1:18,19, "I pray also that the eyes of your heart may be enlightened in order that you may know the hope to which he has called you, the riches of his glorious inheritance in the saints, and his incomparably great power for us who believe." We have no witness when we are living in the flesh. Trying to get defeated young Christians to share their faith is counterproductive. What can they witness about? Only their defeat!

The second reason some young people are ineffective witnesses is because of a lack of focus; they place too much emphasis on temporal things and not enough on eternal relationships. Jesus said, "Watch out! Be on your guard against all kinds of greed; a man's life does not consist in the abundance of his possessions" (Luke 12:15). He then tells a parable about a man who acquired great riches and reasoned that he had enough stored up so that he could eat, drink, and be merry. (See Luke 12:19.) "But God said to him, 'You fool! This very night your life will be demanded from you. Then who will get what you have prepared for yourself?' This is how it will be with anyone who stores up things for himself but is not rich toward God" (Luke 12:20,21).

Man too often seeks happiness and comfort, with no thought for his soul. What would you exchange for love, joy, peace, patience, kindness, goodness, faithfulness, gentleness, and self-control? A new car? A better boyfriend or girlfriend? The lie of Satan is that social status, material possessions, appearance, or other temporal rewards of this world will bring the lasting joy that only God can bring—exchanging the pleasures of the soul for the pleasures of things. Bad choice!

The last reason that many young people are ineffective witnesses is because they don't understand the urgency of evangelism. Wouldn't you drop whatever you were doing to immediately warn a blindfolded child who was walking toward the edge of a cliff? Every day, thousands of Christless feet march toward their eternal death; the loss of eternal life is far greater than the loss of our temporal physical life, which will ultimately be lost anyway.

Jesus appeals to our sense of compassion when He says:

> Suppose one of you has a hundred sheep and loses one of them. Does he not leave the ninety-nine in the open country and go after the lost sheep until he finds it? And when he finds it, he joyfully puts it on his shoulders and goes home. Then he calls his friends and neighbors together and says, "Rejoice with me; I have found my lost sheep." I tell you that in the same way there is more rejoicing in heaven over one sinner who repents than over ninety-nine righteous persons who do not need to repent (Luke 15:4-7).

Nothing is more important than the salvation of one person, and we can have no greater significance than to be a witness.

Remember Paul's instruction to Timothy: "Keep your head in all situations, endure hardship, do the work of an evangelist, discharge all the duties of your ministry" (2 Timothy 4:5).

How would you evaluate your own life and witness?

THE LIE TO REJECT:

> I reject the lie that I am unable to witness or share my faith in Christ.

THE TRUTH TO ACCEPT:

I accept the truth that I am called by Christ to witness, and I am able to successfully share whatever Christ leads me to share.

PRAYER FOR TODAY:

Dear heavenly Father, What a privilege it is to be a personal witness to Your resurrection power within me. Forgive me for the times I have let other things overshadow the value of a lost sheep. And forgive me for placing a higher value on acquiring temporal things than on the value of life itself. I confess that I have sometimes focused on storing up treasures on earth rather than treasures in heaven.

I want to be a witness to the life of Christ within me. I renounce the lies of Satan that say I lack the power or ability to be a credible witness. I pray that You will enable me to be free in Christ so my life will be a witness to Your resurrection power. Open my eyes to the field that is ripe for harvest. Enable me to see the daily opportunities to witness and testify to Your great love. I pray that I will never be a stumbling block to those who are blinded to the gospel. I ask all this in the wonderful name of Jesus my Lord. Amen.

Day Thirty-Five

Behold, I am coming soon! My reward is with me, and I will give to everyone according to what he has done (Revelation 22:12).

Paul said, "Do you not know that in a race all the runners run, but only one gets the prize? Run in such a way as to get the prize" (1 Corinthians 9:24). When we get to heaven and stand before the judgment seat of Christ we will receive a reward, but living free here and now also has its rewards. The prize of freedom is a great reward. What is worth more than peace? What can compare with the inner joy of knowing you're radically right with God? Being free also enables you to make the right decisions. When you're in bondage to a destructive sin, you aren't likely to make good and sound choices. You might have difficulty understanding God's Word or hearing His gentle voice leading you. But when you're free, God's will is easy to discern. He desires close, intimate conversation. He wants to give you guidance in every area of your life. No issue is too big or too small for God.

Living free is a rewarding life because we are under God's protection. When we sin and rebel against God, we move ourselves out from under His loving protection. But when we are free from sin's bondage, God is also free to protect and bless us. Psalm 5:11 says, "Let all who take refuge in you be glad; let them ever sing for joy. Spread your protection over them, that those who love your name may rejoice in you."

Have you seen the EverReady bunny commercials? He just keeps going and going and going. These commercials illustrate an important biblical truth. Why does the bunny have such incredible endurance? Because the source of his strength is reliable and strong. The bunny has the "very best batteries" inside of him.

Like that bunny, you have the strength you need inside. You are now in Christ; the Holy Spirit now indwells you. As you declare your dependence on God, you will find that He will supply you with the endurance and encouragement you need to stay free. Your spiritual life will just keep going and going and going. Not only that, it will keep growing and growing and growing.

> For everything that was written in the past was written to teach us, so that through endurance and the encouragement of the Scriptures we might have hope. May the God who gives endurance and encouragement give you a spirit of unity among yourselves as you follow Christ Jesus, so that with one heart and mouth you may glorify the God and Father of our Lord Jesus Christ (Romans 15:4-6).

You can't just try harder or decide that you're going to be encouraged. God is the source of our encouragement and endurance. He promises to supply these things. The apostle Paul reminded the Colossian believers that they could live a life worthy of the Lord because He would supply strength. "And we pray this in order that you may live a life worthy of the Lord and may please him in every way: bearing fruit in every good work, growing in the knowledge of God, being strengthened with all power according to his glorious might so that you may have great endurance and patience" (Colossians 1:10,11).

We are now free to run from sin and hold onto what is righteous, because God has given us eternal life and a new position in Christ. "But you, man of God, flee from all this, and pursue righteousness, godliness, faith, love, endurance and gentleness. Fight the good fight of the faith. Take hold of the eternal life to which you were called when you made your good confession in the presence of many witnesses" (1 Timothy 6:11,12).

The Bible is full of examples of endurance. After Christ, the apostle Paul is probably the one to be admired the most for his endurance. In his commitment to telling everybody about Jesus, he traveled the world, got shipwrecked and snake-bit, and was repeatedly beaten and stoned for his faith. He didn't seek after a career or even a family. He spent years chained to a Roman guard in prison and eventually was beheaded. Since the following words come from Paul they aren't hard to accept.

> Do you not know that in a race all the runners run, but only one gets the prize? Run in such a way as to get the prize. Everyone who competes in the games goes into strict training. They do it to get a crown that will not last; but we do it to get a crown that will last forever. Therefore I do not run like a man running aimlessly; I do not fight like a man beating the air. No, I beat my body and make it my slave so that after I have preached to others, I myself will not be disqualified for the prize (1 Corinthians 9:24-27).

How is your spiritual endurance?

If you were to stand before Christ right now how would He reward you?

THE LIE TO REJECT:

I reject the lie that I cannot endure and stand strong in Christ during times of trials and tribulations.

THE TRUTH TO ACCEPT:

I accept the truth that I am called by Christ to run a good race, and I am able to do so through the power of the Holy Spirit.

PRAYER FOR TODAY:

Dear heavenly Father, What a privilege to know that I can receive an everlasting crown from You. Lord, I want to have many crowns to place at Your feet! Forgive me for the times I have not run a good race or set my mind on the things of Christ. I confess that I have sometimes run my own race, caring only about going my own way. Lord, I want to run in such a way as to get the prize. I want to be a servant to others. I renounce the lies of Satan that say I lack the power or ability to be a loving servant. I ask all this in the wonderful name of Jesus my Lord. Amen.

εXτrεmε εXτrΑς

εXPLorε τhε Word

Write out what these verses say about you.

(Ephesians 1:5): _____

(Ephesians 2:5,6): _____

(Ephesians 2:18): _____

(Ephesians 3:12): _____

(Colossians 1:13,14): _____

(Colossians 1:27): _____

(Colossians 2:7): _____

εXPΑnd γour mind

Memorize Ephesians 2:4-6:

Because of his great love for us, God, who
is rich in mercy, made us alive with Christ even
when we were dead in transgressions—it is by
grace you have been saved. And God raised us
up with Christ and seated us with him in the
heavenly realms in Christ Jesus.

EXPRESS YOURSELF

8

BEYOND EXTREME
DIRECT ACCESS TO GOD

Day Thirty-Six

He came and preached peace to you who were far away and peace to those who were near. For through him we both have access to the Father by one Spirit (Ephesians 2:17,18).

When I (Neil) was completing my basic training for the U.S. Navy, I was assigned to an evening watch with the officer of the day, a young lieutenant who was quite personable. We had a lot in common, and we enjoyed a pleasant evening chatting together. Still, he represented the ultimate authority on the base, and I was there to do his bidding.

Throughout my four-hour watch, several recruits showed up in his office either for disciplinary reasons or with a request of some kind. Everyone who approached had to "sound off" in a specific way according to naval protocol. If he did it wrong, he had to do it again. In obvious fear, some had to do it again and again until they got it right. They were intimidated by the lieutenant, and they hoped for mercy.

When I reported for duty, I had also approached this authority figure with some fear. However, I quickly realized I had a right to be there, and that it was the safest place on the base as long as I had a good relationship with the lieutenant. My sense of security was dependent upon my obedience to and respect for this authority figure. It was a position I was not about to abuse by becoming disrespectful or disobedient. I also realized that all of the other recruits could have the same sense of safety and security if they were willing to humble themselves and approach him with the respect his position demanded.

There is only one way to approach God—through Jesus Christ, who said, "'I am the way and the truth and the life. No one comes to the Father except through me'" (John 14:6). Jesus is the door; He is the access through whom we have the right to come to the throne of grace. Our only right to be there is because of the shed blood of the Lord Jesus Christ and His grace.

The writer of Hebrews says, "Let us then approach the throne of grace with confidence, so that we may receive mercy and find grace to help us in our time of need" (Hebrews 4:16). Add to that Paul's words: "In him and through faith in him we may approach God with freedom and confidence" (Ephesians 3:12). We have the *right* to come before God, because we are *in Christ*, and Christ is seated at the right hand of our heavenly Father.

Abuse of power and position has left many people fearful of authority figures. Children are afraid to approach their parents, and some youth are afraid of being confronted by a legalistic youth pastor. And so, people often project their human reactions to authority onto their relationship with God. If they can't approach their "under-shepherds," how can they approach God?

But God is not like that. He is love, and the punishment we deserve was placed upon His only Son. This is what John says in his first epistle: "God is love. Whoever lives in love lives in God, and God in him. Love is made complete among us so that we will have confidence on the day of judgment, because in this world we are like him. There is no fear in love. But perfect love drives out fear, because fear has to do with punishment. The man who fears is not made perfect in love" (1 John 4:16-18).

Being afraid of God is not a new problem. In the Old Testament, access to God was forbidden, and people feared His judgment. Only on the Day of Atonement could the high priest alone enter into the holy of holies, and that was an awesome experience. He went through elaborate ceremonial cleansing in order to be qualified to enter. A rope was tied around his leg and bells were hemmed to the bottom of his garment, indicating to those outside that he was still alive in the presence of God. If they no longer heard the bells, they used the rope to pull him out.

Under the former covenant, the way into the sanctuary of God's presence was closed to people, because the blood of animal sacrifices could never completely atone for their sins. Now, however, believers can come to the throne of grace because the perfect priest has offered the perfect sacrifice, atoning for sin once and for all. When Jesus died, the curtain separating the holy place from the Most Holy Place "was torn in two from top to bottom" (Mark 15:38). The curtain symbolizes the body of Christ; His body suffers and is torn to open the way into the divine presence.

The writer of Hebrews beautifully depicts this entrance into God's presence prepared for us by the Lord Jesus Christ:

> Therefore, brothers, since we have confidence to enter the Most Holy Place by the blood of Jesus, by a new and living way opened for us through the curtain, that is, his body, and since we have a great priest over the house of God, let us draw near to God with a sincere heart in full assurance of faith, having our hearts sprinkled to cleanse us from a guilty conscience and having our bodies washed with pure water. Let us hold unswervingly to the hope we profess, for he who promised is faithful. And let us

consider how we may spur one another on toward love and good deeds (Hebrews 10:19-24).

The Lie to Reject:

I reject the lie of Satan that says God doesn't love me and that I don't have any right to be in His presence.

The Truth to Accept:

I accept the truth that I can boldly approach Your throne with my heart cleansed by the blood of Jesus, and find mercy and grace in time of need.

Prayer for Today:

Dear heavenly Father, You are holy and in complete control of the universe, and I acknowledge Your authority. I come before Your presence by way of the shed blood of the Lord Jesus Christ. I acknowledge that I have no other right on my own to be in Your presence. I honor You as the Lord of my life. I place my trust in You and commit myself to obey You. Because of Your love, I no longer fear punishment. Instead, I seek Your presence as the only place of safety and security. I renounce the lies of Satan that say You do not love me or that I don't have a right to be in Your presence. I come to You in freedom and in confidence, with a sincere heart, in full assurance of faith. In Jesus' precious name I pray. Amen.

Day Thirty-Seven

In him and through faith in him we may approach God with freedom and confidence (Ephesians 3:12).

Suppose you entered a youth contest that was offering the winner an all-expenses-paid trip to Washington, D.C.. The trip included a 15-minute private session in the Oval Office of the White House with the president of the United States. You could ask any question and tell him anything you wanted to tell him. This would certainly be one of the most significant days of your life.

You would probably want to videotape the event, so you could watch it over and over. The glory of the moment would quickly fade, so you would also want a picture of you and the president to commemorate the occasion. You could hang it on your bedroom wall and show all your friends and relatives. After all, how many people have experienced such a privilege and honor? Many influential leaders would pay handsomely for a private audience with the president.

You would undoubtedly experience a few anxious moments as you tried to figure out what to say and ask. It wouldn't take long to realize, however, that what you did say would have little, if any, lasting impact on the course of history. The president would, of course, be polite and treat you cordially. After all, there is a little publicity value in this for him also—the president of the United States rubbing shoulders with youth, showing that he is interested in listening to what young people have to say.

Are you aware that we have already won a far better prize? An all-expenses-paid trip to heaven is ours, and included in the package is a private audience with the one who *created* the president of the United States and all the other world leaders. What's more, we are assured that the encounter will have eternal and lasting consequences. Every child of God, young and old, has received the same prize, yet few bother to even claim it!

We have free access to the God of the universe, 24 hours of every day. He has no office hours, and He never grows weary of our need for personal time with Him. How can this be? Because Jesus paid the price; He made the provision! "For through him we both have access to the Father by one Spirit" (Ephesians 2:18).

We have a tendency to check in with God only during a crisis. In the ball game of life, prayer should be a first-down huddle to ask for direction, not a fourth-down punting situation. When we pray according to the Holy Spirit's prompting, we can be assured that God the Father will answer in our best interest:

> In the same way, the Spirit helps us in our weakness. We do not know what we ought to pray, but the Spirit himself intercedes for us with groans that words cannot express. And he who searches our hearts knows the mind of the Spirit, because the Spirit intercedes for the saints in accordance with God's will (Romans 8:26,27).

Primarily, what we try to determine in prayer is God's will. After addressing our Father in heaven, the Lord's prayer continues with, "Your kingdom come, your will be done on earth as it is in heaven" (Matthew 6:10). Sometimes the will of God includes suffering, so Paul said to the Ephesians, "I ask you, therefore, not to be discouraged because of my sufferings for you, which are your glory" (Ephesians 3:13). Sometimes God's will appears to dash our hopes and dreams.

In prayer, we are also dependent upon the Holy Spirit to open our eyes. The Holy Spirit will lead us into all truth and keep us in God's will. And remember, Jesus has provided you free access to the heavenly Father; you can have a private audience with Him 24 hours of every day for the rest of your eternal life.

THE LIE TO REJECT:

I reject the lie of Satan that says I am just a number or a face in the crowd to God.

THE TRUTH TO ACCEPT:

I accept the truth that in Christ I am able to personally spend time with God and know Him intimately.

PRAYER FOR TODAY:

Make this prayer from Ephesians 3:14-19 your own by inserting your name in it:

Dear heavenly Father, from whom Your whole family in heaven and on earth derives its name I, (name), kneel before You. I pray that out of Your glorious riches You may strengthen me, (name), with power through Your Spirit, so that Christ may dwell in my heart through faith. And I pray that I, (name), may have power, together with all the saints, to grasp how wide and long and high and deep is the love of Christ, and to know this love that passes knowledge—that I, (name), may be filled to the measure of all Your fullness. In Your Son's name I pray. Amen.

Day Thirty-Eight

Let us then approach the throne of grace with confidence, so that we may receive mercy and find grace to help us in our time of need (Hebrews 4:16).

How can God possibly understand our struggles? He sits up there in the heavenlies, all powerful and all wise. He doesn't have any needs. He doesn't worry about passing any test. He doesn't have an abusive parent. He wasn't born on the wrong side of the tracks.

The answer is in Jesus. His family suffered from the social rejection of an unexplainable birth. He was rejected by His countrymen. He took upon Himself the form of a man with no special privileges. He had no class status, no possessions. He carried the cross for His own crucifixion. He was cursed, beaten, and spat upon. And to add final humiliation:

One of the criminals who hung there hurled insults at him: "Aren't you the Christ? Save yourself and us!" But the other criminal rebuked him. "Don't you fear God," he said, "since you are under the same sentence? We are punished justly, for we are getting what our deeds deserve. But this man has done nothing wrong" (Luke 23:39,40).

Jesus didn't deserve punishment and death—we did! Do we actually think He lacks understanding and is unmerciful? "Let us fix our eyes on Jesus, the author and perfecter of our faith, who for the joy set before him endured the cross, scorning its shame, and sat down at the right hand of the throne of God. Consider him who endured such opposition from sinful men, so that you will not grow weary and lose heart" (Hebrews 12:2,3).

Yes, you can turn to God for mercy and grace! If you have any doubt, Hebrews 4:14-16 settles it:

> Therefore, since we have a great high priest who has gone through the heavens, Jesus the Son of God, let us hold firmly to the faith we profess. For we do not have a high priest who is unable to sympathize with our weaknesses, but we have one who has been tempted in every way, just as we are—yet was without sin. Let us then approach the throne of grace with confidence, so that we may receive mercy and find grace to help us in our time of need.

One Christmas Eve, I (Neil) received a special gift from a lady who had experienced unspeakable atrocities during her childhood. The gift was a letter to me written in the form of a parable. It beautifully captures the message and ministry of the church. Let me share it with you:

> While on vacation as a child one year, I happened upon a gold watch that was lying face down in the parking lot of our motel. It was covered with dirt and gravel. At first glance, it did not seem worth the effort to bend down and pick it up, but for some reason I found myself reaching for it anyway.

The crystal was broken, the watchband was gone, and there was moisture on the dial. From all appearances, there was no logical reason to believe this watch would still work. Every indication was that its next stop would be the trash can.

Those in my family who were with me at the time laughed at me for picking it up. My mother even scolded me for holding such a dirty object that was so obviously destroyed. As I reached for the winding stem, my brother made a comment about my lack of intelligence.

"It's been run over by cars," he chided. "Nothing can endure that kind of treatment!"

As I turned the stem, the second hand of the watch began to move. My family was wrong. Truly, odds were against the watch working, but there was one thing no one thought of. No matter how broken the outside was, if the inside was not damaged, it would still run, and indeed it did keep perfect time. This watch was made to keep time. Its outside appearance had nothing to do with the purpose for which it was designed. Although the appearance was damaged, the inside was untouched and in perfect condition.

Twenty-five years later, I still have that watch. I take it out every once in a while and wind it up, and it still works. I think as long as the inside remains untouched, it always will. However, unless I had bothered to pick it up and try to wind it years ago, I never would have known the part that really mattered was still in perfect condition. Although it looks like a piece of junk, it will always be a treasure to me, because I looked beyond the outside appearance and believed in what really mattered, it's ability to function in the manner for which it was created.

Thank you, Neil for making the effort to "pick up the watch," and "turn the stem." You are helping me to see that my emotions may be damaged but my inner self is still in perfect condition, and that is what was created to be with Christ. The only permanent part. The part that really mattered. I know that deep within my heart, no matter what my feelings are telling me, this is true. I also believe that with the help of God's servants, even the "casing" can be repaired, and maybe even that will become functional again.

People all over the world are being damaged everyday. Desperate youth are crying out for mercy and grace. We have the privilege to "pick up the watch" and "turn the stem." But we have to look beyond the casing. Then we can extend God's mercy and grace and connect these people to God. God has made a wonderful provision for our recovery: Every hour of every day and for all eternity, we can go to our Great High Priest and receive mercy and grace in our time of need. Where does our confidence lie? "Therefore, brothers, since we have confidence to enter the Most Holy Place by the blood of Jesus, . . . let us draw near to God with a sincere heart in full assurance of faith" (Hebrews 10:19,22).

THE LIE TO REJECT:

I reject the lie of Satan that distorts the knowledge of who God really is, and how He can relate to and care for me.

THE TRUTH TO ACCEPT:

I accept the truth that Christ always knows what I'm going through, and I am always allowed to experience His love and presence.

PRAYER FOR TODAY:

Dear heavenly Father, forgive me for not coming first to You, and for questioning whether You could really understand my needs. Thank You for Your mercy. I know I don't deserve it and neither do I deserve Your grace, but I praise You because You are a gracious God. I renounce the lies of Satan that distort the knowledge of who You really are. Teach me to be merciful to others as You are merciful to me, and teach me to give people what they need, not what they deserve. I thank You for Jesus Christ, who made it possible for me to come before Your presence, and I resolve from this day forward to do just that. I praise You for Your mercy and grace and for Your open invitation for me to come to You. In Jesus' precious name I pray. Amen.

DAY THIRTY-NINE

But our citizenship is in heaven. And we eagerly await a Savior from there, the Lord Jesus Christ (Philippians 3:20).

The car radio blared out the news. The trial of the four policemen accused of beating Rodney King was over, and tensions were already high in the city due to deteriorating race relations, gang wars, and high unemployment. When the news hit that the policemen were acquitted, the world witnessed the total disintegration of society in Los Angeles for the next two days. The city was a ghostly sight! Smoke from thousands of fires filled the sky. It was like a war zone. The freeways were strangely empty. It was anarchy, a sickening demonstration of the sinful ways of man. College students in expensive cars joined in the madness. Looters were grabbing all they could get.

The whole scene mirrored something Paul wrote in Philippians 3:18-20, "As I have often told you before and now say again even with tears, many live as enemies of the cross of Christ. Their destiny is destruction, their god is their stomach, and their glory is in their shame. Their mind is on earthly things. But our citizenship is in heaven." We are in this world, but we are not of it. Paul continues, "And we eagerly await a Savior from there, the Lord Jesus Christ, who, by the power that enables him to bring everything under his control, will transform our lowly bodies so that they will be like his glorious body" (verses 20,21).

It is little wonder that the citizens of this world feel so insecure. Stress is a leading cause of physical illness.

More money is spent on the temporary cures for anxiety than on any other consumer need. Young people and adults alike mask their pain with prescription drugs or escape through alcohol, drugs, sex, and food. Any many of the young people who realize those habits are destructive, so they devote their lives to the preservation and glorification of their physical bodies.

Our hope doesn't lie in the false assurance that we will never die, but rather in the resurrection, as Paul describes in Romans 8:23,24: "Not only so, but we ourselves, who have the firstfruits of the Spirit, groan inwardly as we wait eagerly for our adoption as sons, the redemption of our bodies. For in this hope we were saved."

Peter talks about the days before the second coming of Christ. He warns us that there will be scoffers who will mock the possibility of a second coming. He talks about the sudden destruction that will come upon us. But in the midst of his warnings, he encourages us:,

> But do not forget this one thing, dear friends: With the Lord a day is like a thousand years, and a thousand years are like a day. The Lord is not slow in keeping his promise, as some understand slowness. He is patient with you, not wanting anyone to perish, but everyone to come to repentance (2 Peter 3:8,9).

God is waiting for the gospel to be preached to all the nations; then the end will come. We are not of this world, but we are left here for a purpose: We are to fulfill His Great Commission. When the gospel has gone out to the ends of the world, He will return.

So don't wear your citizenship in heaven as a badge of superiority. We are all saved by the grace of God. No matter how sick and depraved the fallen humanity around you may appear, always remember the sober reminder: "There, but for the grace of God, go I." Our heavenly citizenship is the basis for hope and security, which carries with it the responsibility to be servants of God, subservient to His will. We have been left on earth for a purpose. As Peter writes, "Dear friends, I urge you, as aliens and strangers in the world, to abstain from sinful desires, which war against your soul. Live such good lives among the pagans that, though they accuse you of doing wrong, they may see your good deeds and glorify God on the day he visits us" (1 Peter 2:11,12).

The Lie to Reject:

I reject the lie of Satan that says my only citizenship is on earth and not in heaven.

The Truth to Accept:

I accept the truth that I have rights and responsibilities as a citizen of heaven, and declare Jesus to be my King.

Prayer for Today:

Dear heavenly Father, I thank You for my citizenship in heaven. Forgive me for the times that I have sought my security in this world, and lived as though I have no eternal relationship with You. I renounce the lie of Satan that says my only citizenship is on earth and not in heaven. I now claim my rights and responsibilities as a citizen of heaven, and declare You to be my King. I commit myself to be Your servant and to do Your will on earth as it is being done in heaven. My hope is not in this present world, but in the one to come. I will seek to live a responsible life today, so that, by Your grace, the world may see my good deeds and thereby glorify You. In Jesus' precious name I pray. Amen.

Day Forty

Being confident of this, that he who began a good work in you will carry it on to completion until the day of Christ Jesus (Philippians 1:6).

I remember hearing about the famous guard for the Green Bay Packers, Jerry Krammer, talking about his first year on the team. He was a rookie and the great coach, Vince Lombardi, was riding him constantly. When the rest of the team was excused for the day, Krammer was ordered to do another 20 minutes' running through the tire obstacle course! Frustrated and defeated, the player went into the locker room and contemplated quitting the team.

At Jerry's lowest moment, the coach walked by and thumped him on the back of the helmet. "Someday, Krammer," he said, "you are going to be the greatest guard football has ever known." Vince Lombardi was known for riding his people to perfection, but he was also a master of timing. Jerry says about that moment : "I went from complete despair to total ecstasy, willing to do whatever the coach might require, even another 20 minutes on the tires."

In Matthew 8:23-26, we read this account:

> Then he got into the boat and his disciples followed him. Without warning, a furious storm came up on the lake, so that the waves swept over the boat. But Jesus was sleeping. The disciples went and woke him, saying, "Lord, save us! We're going to drown!"
>
> He replied, "You of little faith, why are you so afraid?" Then he got up and rebuked the winds and the waves, and it was completely calm.

There is no way that boat would ever sink with Jesus in it; it was destined to make it to the other side. Though storms rage around us, we are destined to make it to the other side because Christ is in us—He is our hope of glory. It is He who has begun the work in us, and He will carry it on to completion.

Another story involving Jesus and a boat is found in Mark 6:45-50:

> And immediately He made His disciples get into the boat and go ahead of Him to the other side to Bethsaida, while He Himself was sending the multitude away. And after bidding them farewell, He departed to the mountain to pray. And when it was evening, the boat was in the midst of the sea, and He was alone on the land. And seeing them straining at the oars, for the wind was against them, at about the fourth

watch of the night, He came to them, walking
on the sea; and He intended to pass by them.
But when they saw Him walking on the sea,
they supposed that it was a ghost, and cried
out; for they all saw Him and were frightened.
But immediately He spoke with them and said
to them, "Take courage; it is I, do not be afraid"
(NASB).

Look at the phrase, "He intended to pass by them." I
believe that even today Jesus intends to pass by the
self-sufficient. If we think getting to the other side is
determined by how hard we row, we may never get
there. We must never forget that it is He who began the
work in us, and it is He who will carry it to completion.

A retired grandfather arrived late for a Little League
game and stopped to ask his grandchild how his team
was doing. "We are behind 15 to nothing," he said.

The grandfather asked, "Are you discouraged?"

"Of course not," the boy responded. "We haven't
been up to bat yet."

We can have that kind of confidence because we
know the Lord is working in us.

I don't know which "inning" of life you are in, but
the odds are you have at least one more opportunity to
come to the plate. Are you running against the wind?
Have you failed in the past? Do you believe God has
given up on you? I don't believe He has! In Philippians
3:12-14, Paul reflects the attitude we must have if we
want to win:

Not that I have already obtained all this, or
have already been made perfect, but I press on
to take hold of that for which Christ Jesus took

hold of me. Brothers, I do not consider myself yet to have taken hold of it. But one thing I do: Forgetting what is behind and straining toward what is ahead, I press on toward the goal to win the prize for which God has called me heavenward in Christ Jesus.

The Lie to Reject:

I reject the lie of Satan that says God is finished with me. I renounce my self-sufficiency, and I choose to forget what lies behind.

The Truth to Accept:

I accept the truth that Jesus who began a good work in me will complete the whole task of making me like Him.

Prayer for Today:

Dear heavenly Father, I am thankful for the good work You have begun in me. I know You are not finished with me yet, and I renounce the lie of Satan that would suggest that You are. Forgive me for the times I have lived in my own sufficiency. I renounce my self-sufficiency, and I choose to forget what lies behind. I now commit myself to press on to Your upward call and express with confidence that I shall see You face-to-face on the other side. I put no confidence in the flesh, for my confidence lies in You. You will bring me to completion in Christ. In Jesus' precious name I pray. Amen.

EXTREME EXTRAS

EXPLORE THE WORD

Write out what these verses say about you.

(Colossians 2:10,12,13): _____

(Colossians 3:1-4): _____

(2 Timothy 1:7,9): _____

(Hebrews 2:11): _____

(Hebrews 4:16): _____

(2 Peter 1:4): _____

EXPAND YOUR MIND

Memorize Hebrews 4:16:

Let us then approach the throne of grace
with confidence, so that we may receive mercy
and find grace to help us in our time of need.

EXPRESS YOURSELF

---

12 Extra Days of Extreme Faith

Don't stop now! Here are 12 extra days that will help you walk free in Christ. Continue in God's word by reading these key verses and selecting sections of Scripture to memorize. Be sure to express what God is saying about you in these verses. Writing down these verses and what they mean to you will help you remember them and find additional insights.

Day 1:   1 Corinthians 6:17
Day 2:   1 Corinthians 6:19,20
Day 3:   1 Corinthians 12:27
Day 4:   Colossians 1:13,14
Day 5:   Proverbs 3:19-26
Day 6:   Romans 8: 31-34
Day 7:   1 Corinthians 3:9; 4:1,2
Day 8:   Matthew 5:13-16
Day 9:   John 15:1-5
Day 10: John 15:16,17
Day 11: 1 Corinthians 3:16,17
Day 12: Ephesians 2:10

> "Understanding your identity in Christ is
> absolutely essential to your success at living
> the victorious Christian life!"

Who am I?

I am accepted . . .

John 1:12	I am God's child.
John 15:15	I am Christ's friend.
Rom. 5:1	I have been justified.
1 Cor. 6:17	I am united with the Lord, and I am one spirit with Him.
1 Cor. 6:19,20	I have been bought with a price. I belong to God.
1 Cor. 12:27	I am a member of Christ's body.
Eph. 1:1	I am a saint.
Eph. 1:5	I have been adopted as God's child.
Eph. 2:18	I have direct access to God through the Holy Spirit.
Col. 1:14	I have been redeemed and forgiven of all my sins.
Col. 2:10	I am complete in Christ.

I am secure . . .

Rom. 8:1,2	I am free forever from condemnation.
Rom. 8:28	I am assured that all things work together for good.
Rom. 8:31f	I am free from any condemning charges against me.
Rom. 8:35f	I cannot be separated from the love of God.
2 Cor. 1:21,22	I have been established, anointed, and sealed by God.
Col. 3:3	I am hidden with Christ in God.
Phil. 1:6	I am confident that the good work that God has begun in me will be perfected.
Phil. 3:20	I am a citizen of heaven.
2 Tim. 1:7	I have not been given a spirit of fear but of power, love, and a sound mind.
Heb. 4:16	I can find grace and mercy in time of need.
1 John 5:18	I am born of God, and the evil one cannot touch me.

I am significant . . .

Matt. 5:13,14	I am the salt and light of the earth.
John 15:1,5	I am a branch of the true vine, a channel of His life.
Acts 1:8	I am a personal witness of Christ's.
1 Cor. 3:16	I am God's temple.
2 Cor. 5:17f	I am a minister of reconciliation for God.
2 Cor. 6:1	I am God's coworker (1 Cor. 3:9).
Eph. 2:6	I am seated with Christ in the heavenly realm.
Eph. 2:10	I am God's workmanship.
Eph. 3:12	I may approach God with freedom and confidence.
Phil. 4:13	I can do all things through Christ who strengthens me.

(From "Living Free in Christ" by Dr. Neil Anderson)

40 Daily Scripture Readings for Luke

DAY 1	1:1-56	John's and Jesus' birth foretold
DAY 2	1:57–2:20	The advent of John and Jesus
DAY 3	2:21-52	The baby Jesus and Jesus as a boy
DAY 4	3:1-38	Baptism and background of Jesus
DAY 5	4:1-30	Jesus' temptation and purpose
DAY 6	4:31-44	Jesus authority over demons and disease
DAY 7	5:1-26	Jesus and the disciples and the unclean
DAY 8	5:27-39	Jesus and the wineskin parable
DAY 9	6:1-11	Jesus and healing on the Sabbath
DAY 10	6:12-49	The call and exhortation of the disciples
DAY 11	7:1-35	Jesus heals sickness and raises the dead
DAY 12	7:36-50	Jesus and the sinners
DAY 13	8:1-21	Jesus and sowing and lampstand parables
DAY 14	8:22-39	Jesus, authority over nature and the demonic
DAY 15	8:40-56	Jesus and despair
DAY 16	9:1-17	Jesus uses the disciples for God's glory
DAY 17	9:18-62	Jesus tells about His death
DAY 18	10:1-24	Call of the seventy-two
DAY 19	10:25-42	The good Samaritan; Mary and Martha
DAY 20	11:1-54	How to pray and Jesus rejected
DAY 21	12:1-34	Hypocrisy and covetousness
DAY 22	12:35-59	Faithfulness and the signs
DAY 23	13:1-35	Repentance and the kingdom
DAY 24	14:1-35	Jesus and the people
DAY 25	15:1-32	Jesus, love for sinners
DAY 26	16:1-31	Jesus talks about money
DAY 27	17:1-19	Forgiveness, service, and gratitude
DAY 28	17:20-37	Jesus and the kingdom
DAY 29	18:1-14	Jesus and prayer
DAY 30	18:15-30	Getting in the kingdom
DAY 31	18:31–19:10	Jesus predicts His death; salvation
DAY 32	19:11-27	Faithfulness
DAY 33	19:28-48	Not your average Sunday and Monday
DAY 34	20:1-47	Jesus' authority requested, revealed, rejected
DAY 35	21:1-38	Signs of the End Times
DAY 36	22:1-53	Last Supper, garden, arrest
DAY 37	22:54-71	Jesus denied and beaten
DAY 38	23:1-56	Jesus mocked, crucified, buried
DAY 39	24:1-35	Jesus' victory over death
DAY 40	24:36-53	Jesus appears, encourages His disciples and you

NOTES

Chapter 3

1. Rich Miller, "Truth About Our Heavenly Father," unpublished ms.
2. Floyd McClung, Jr., *The Father Heart of God* (Eugene, OR: Harvest House Publishers, 1985), pp. 111-14.

Chapter 4

1. Charles Swindoll, *Christian Life* (Portland, OR: Multnomah Press, 1986), pp. 177-278.
2. Neil Anderson and Dave Park, *Stomping Out the Darkness* (Ventura, CA: Regal Books, 1993), pp. 101-02.

Chapter 6

1. Statistics released by the Children's Defense Fund, Jan. 8, 1990.
2. Erwin Lutzers, *How in This World Can I Be Holy?* (Chicago: Moody Press, 1979), pp. 7-8.

Other Books by Neil and Dave

Bondage Breaker, Youth Edition
Bondage Breaker, Youth Edition Study Guide
Stomping Out the Darkness
Stomping Out the Darkness, Study Guide
Busting Free, Youth Curriculum

Freedom in Christ 4 Teens

Devotional Series

Extreme Faith
by Neil T. Anderson and Dave Park
Reality Check
by Neil T. Anderson and Rich Miller

Other Youth Resources from Freedum in Christ

To My Dear Slimeball
by Rich Miller
Know Him, No Fear
by Rich Miller and Neil Anderson

Freedom in Christ Youth Conferences

Stomping Out the Darkness
For high school and junior high students

Setting Your Youth Free
For adults who serve youth

Purity Under Pressure
For high school and junior high students

For more information about having a
Freedom in Christ youth event in your area, call or write:

Freedom in Christ Youth Ministries
491 E. Lambert Road
La Habra, CA 90631
(310) 691-9128

Freedom in Christ Ministries

Purpose: *Freedom in Christ Ministries is an interdenomiational, international, Bible-teaching Church ministry which exists to glorify God by equipping churches and mission groups, enabling them to fulfill their mission of establishing people free in Christ.*

Freedom in Christ Ministries offers a number of valuable video, audio, and print resources that will help both those in need and those who counsel. Among the topics covered are:

Resolving Personal Conflicts

Search for Identity ■ *Walking by Faith* ■ *Faith Renewal* ■ *Renewing the Mind* ■ *Battle for the Mind* ■ *Emotions* ■ *Relationships* ■ *Forgiveness*

Resolving Spiritual Conflicts

Position of Believer ■ *Authority* ■ *Protection* ■ *Vulnerability* ■ *Temptation* ■ *Accusation* ■ *Deception & Discernment* ■ *Steps to Freedom*

Spiritual Conflicts and Biblical Counseling

Biblical Integration ■ *Theological Basis* ■ *Walking by the Spirit* ■ *Surviving the Crisis* ■ *The Process of Growth* ■ *Counseling and Christ* ■ *Counseling the Spiritually Afflicted* ■ *Ritual Abuse*

The Seduction of Our Children

God's Answer ■ *Identity and Self-Worth* ■ *Styles of Communication* ■ *Discipline* ■ *Spiritual Conflicts and Prayer* ■ *Steps to Freedom*

Resolving Spiritual Conflicts and Cross-Cultural Ministry
Dr. Timothy Warner

Worldview Problems ■ *Warfare Relationships* ■ *Christians and Demons* ■ *The Missionary Under Attack* ■ *Practical Application for Missionaries* ■ *Steps to Freedom in Christ*